CHICK LIVING™

Frugal and Fabulous

KRIS KOEDERITZ MELCHER

CONARI PRESS

First published in 2005 by Conari Press,

an imprint of Red Wheel/Weiser, LLC
York Beach, ME
With offices at:
368 Congress Street
Boston, MA 02210

www.redwheelweiser.com

Library of Congress Cataloging-in-Publication Data available upon request.

Typeset in ITC Century Book, by Anne Carter
Printed in Canada
TCP
12 11 10 09 08 07 06 05
  8 7 6 5 4 3 2 1

For Isabella, my favorite little chick.
May all your dreams come true.

CONTENTS

ACKNOWLEDGMENTS

This book would not have been possible without the help of several people. Thanks to Jan Johnson and Brenda Knight at Conari for the opportunity to do this project and for their unwavering enthusiasm; my fabulous editor Kate Hartke; my dear friend and mentor Arnie Fenner; my husband and No. 1 fan Jeff; all of my chick girlfriends—you know who you are; and finally, my parents for their unconditional love and support for thirtysomething years.

I've come a long way since "The Worm."

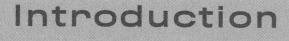

Introduction

WHEN I TOLD MY FATHER THE
SALARY I'D BEEN OFFERED FOR MY
FIRST JOB OUT OF COLLEGE AS A PUBLIC
relations associate for a not-for-profit agency—$18,000—his
response was, "But that's just for the first six months, right?"

Uh, no. That was the salary for the first *year*. I'd done well in
college, graduated from a respected journalism school, and had
a number of PR internships under my belt to boot. But there was
a recession, and companies don't tend to toss six-figure salaries
a recent college graduate's way anyway. In fact, I felt pretty
lucky just to have a job offer, period. I took small consolation in
the fact that most of my friends were in the same boat. Misery
loves company, and at least we could all struggle together.

My ever-optimistic mother and I sat down and created a budget
based on my salary. We were pretty thorough. I decided that if I
took the job, the worst case scenario was that I would be able
to live on my own, get experience, pay all of my bills, save a little money, and even have some fun. If I didn't take the job, the
worst case scenario was that I wouldn't get experience, couldn't

pay my bills, would have to live with my parents, and would probably be too poor and miserable to have fun.

So I took the job. Once out on my own, I figured stuff out through research, trial and error (read: mistakes), friends, and plenty of late-night phone calls to my folks. Some stuff I still haven't figured out. I got my own apartment and decorated it, paid all of my bills on time, put together a Grown-up Girl wardrobe, entertained frequently, and had fun. And I still managed to save $1,000 on that first year's salary. After a year, I got a better job in my field, moved into a nicer apartment, and began to turn my savings into investing.

Whether you're starting a career, getting your first place, trying to manage your moolah, hosting a party, or wanting to look fabulous—all while having to be frugal—I hope I can help. I'm not your mother, your doctor, your boss, your shrink, your conscience, your financial adviser, or your warden. I'm just your girlfriend who's been there, done that, made some mistakes, and learned a little bit along the way.

So for those of you who are just venturing out on your own into the Real World, I raise my dirty martini (with three olives) to you in a toast of congratulations. It's going to be a fabulous journey. Cheers!

—Kris

1

Getting, Keeping, and Advancing at the Job You Want

The big secret in life is
that there is no big secret.
Whatever your goal, you can get
there if you're willing to work.

—OPRAH WINFREY

WHEN I WAS AMONG A TON OF OTHER APPLICANTS FOR A POSITION AT A LARGE INTERNATIONAL PUBLIC relations agency, I knew I had to stand out and that creative writing would be viewed favorably. So I began my cover letter with, "When I was asked to pose for *Playboy*, I was a little nervous." My letter went on to explain that in order to get an interview with world-renowned photographer David Chan, I had shown up for *Playboy*'s "Girls of the Big Eight" photo session. I described waiting in the snow for seven hours alongside many scantily clad, legs-to-here bunny wannabes. I went on to say that although I did not pose for *Playboy*, I did get the interview—and the story. I wrote that it was this kind of tenacity and determination that made me a great candidate for their company. It was a risky move, but one I was comfortable with. And you know what? I was called a few days later and told that it was my cover letter that got their attention and made them want to interview me. I got the job.

So, congratulations! You already have your first job and you don't even know it. It's *looking* for a job—and you're the boss.

Treat the job-search process like the 8-5 responsibility that it is. Get up early, get dressed, grab your mocha latte, and get out there. Don't slack off and don't get discouraged—your diligence will pay off even if it's not quite according to your time frame.

SO, WHAT DO YOU WANT TO DO WITH THE REST OF YOUR LIFE?

Maybe you're one of those lucky people who has known since you were six that you wanted to be an astronaut, and now you're working for NASA. If so, that's fabulous. But if not, it's important to have a heart-to-heart with yourself before looking for a job. Whether you've graduated from college or a vocational or trade school, you probably have *some* idea of what you'd like to do with your training and education, even if you need a little guidance. Figure out your wants, values, interests, personality, skills, abilities, preferences, strengths, weaknesses, and goals. Do you enjoy being around people or prefer the companionship of rats in a lab? Are you good with numbers or do you shudder at the memory of eighth-grade algebra? Are you creative or is your idea of walking on the wild side writing with blue ink instead of black? Write it all down. And be *honest*. Really, really honest. Or a future employer might be—and they may not sugarcoat it.

To get in touch with your inner thoughts, daydream for a moment. Let go of job titles, doubts, self-imposed limitations, salary expectations, and other practical considerations. What kinds of jobs appeal to you? If you follow your heart, you're far more likely to find a job that you love, regardless of how much you're paid.

It's difficult for anyone to be objective about herself, so ask others what they think. Classmates, fellow employees, friends, professors, mentors, former employers, even family can provide you with a valuable assessment.

There are even personality tests, such as Myers-Briggs, that many employers use to help them evaluate potential employees. (If only potential boyfriends could be given such a test!) Check for some of these tests online or see if a career counseling center on your college campus administers these. You may be surprised what you learn about yourself!

Discovering the type of environment you want to work in will help you with the next step of actually choosing your field. For example, if you write about yourself, "English major, loves books, writes well, prefers to work alone in a quiet room," you might choose to look for an editorial position in publishing.

Once you've chosen the field in which you want to work, throw yourself into it. Keep an eye out for the major players by reading industry rags and mags, visiting industry Web sites, participating in professional organizations, and attending "group love" sessions like conferences and seminars. You'll not only *impress* prospective employers with your knowledge, but you might even *find* them through this process as well.

BE A WOMAN OF EXPERIENCE

You know the old saying: You can't get a job without experience, and you can't get experience without a job. But, you *can* get great experience, acquire valuable skills, and make important contacts without getting a job.

GET CLOSE TO YOUR FIELD

Once you know the field you want to pursue, look for any opportunities in it. Work as an office assistant for your particular vocation, even if it's for minimum wage. If you want to be a pharmacist, work in a drugstore. If you want to go into hotel and restaurant management, work as a hotel desk clerk or wait tables in a restaurant. If you want to juggle flaming batons, join the circus.

I once had my sights set on law school, but a gig as an office assistant at a law firm after my freshman year of college changed my mind. While I worked with great people and gained valuable professional experience, I also eventually realized that part of what had made me want to be an attorney was the vision of myself smartly dressed in a suit striding into court carrying my briefcase and looking very important. Nevertheless, the experience proved valuable because all of the research and writing I did for the firm taught me that I had a passion for journalism. I selected Journalism as my major and have loved being in the field ever since.

INTERN

The only way to *really* explore a new occupation is to experience it firsthand. Internships are a great way to get real job experience, build your résumé, establish contacts, and possibly make a little money (some are paid, but the most coveted ones often are not). Treat your internship like the Real Job that it is, and it could lead to a permanent Real Job. Employers are generally lazy about the hiring process because it's stressful, difficult, and time-consuming. If there's someone terrific right under their nose—you—they'd much rather hire that person than have to go out and search for someone else. If you didn't intern somewhere in college, don't sweat it. It's not too late. Many people also do internships after college. Check with your alma mater's career center or call the Human Resources department of companies that interest you and ask about their internship programs.

TRY A TEMP AGENCY

Another great way to get experience, connections, and be paid is to work for a temp agency. These jobs are often flexible and as the name implies, temporary, but they can lead to permanent spots. Some companies use temps to cover absences or assist during a peak period, but more and more people are using their temp jobs as a stepping stone to a permanent position. Temp jobs offer a trial period for both the employee and employer to see if there's a fit. In most cases, the fee is paid to the temp agency by the employer, but make sure this is the case before you sign up. Check to see how long the agency has been in business, and check with your local Better Business Bureau to see if any complaints have been lodged against it. Make an effort to find out how an agency goes about finding its employees. Don't limit yourself to just one agency—register with several if they're reputable.

FREELANCE

Freelance workers are hired for a specific project and usually paid a set fee or hourly rate. For example, publishing companies often hire a graphic designer to create a particular book cover or a copyeditor to review a manuscript. Sometimes a freelance job can turn into a full-time position in a company.

VOLUNTEER

No one turns away free, good help. Volunteering is usually for a good cause, so you'll feel good about yourself, too. If you want to be a P.E. teacher, coach a Little League team. If you're a journalism major, offer to write a newsletter for a not-for-profit organization and ask that they only cover the cost of materials. If you want to be a veterinarian, walk and wash pooches at the local animal shelter. In addition to joining committees and organizations of interest, apply for board positions. While they can be demanding of your time and talents, a board position is *très* impressive on a résumé and will give you great experience and contacts.

 GET CONNECTED

Talk to *everyone, everywhere, all the time.* Put the word out (tactfully, of course) on every occasion. Well, except funerals. Weddings, parties, reunions, happy hours, and your parents' dull dinner parties are all fair game in order to get ahead. Aunt Bertha's second cousin's neighbor's accountant just might have a lead. You never know.

Mark McGurren, vice president of Corporate Personnel and Associates, an executive search and job placement firm, suggests compiling a file of all potential business contacts. "Put together an ongoing 'career Rolodex' of any and all potential employment opportunities, and keep it updated," advises McGurren.

YOUR CALLING CARD

Have your own business cards printed with the important 411—your name, area of expertise, snail mail address, e-mail address, and phone number—and hand them out. You can do these yourself or inexpensively at office supply centers. For an extra polished look that will impress, create your own logo using your initials. You can do this in a simple Word program by playing with fonts, sizes, outlines, shadows, character spacing, and other formatting options. Or find a piece of clip art that attractively and professionally illustrates the first initial of your last name. You can also put this logo on your résumé. Just keep it simple and clean.

JANE DOE
COPY EDITING·WRITING
STREET ADDRESS
CITY, STATE ZIP
TEL (555) 555 5555
E-MAIL ADDRESS

Keep these cards with you all the time—in your pockets, purse, wallet, planner, etc. When you give one to someone, write a note on it. Something like, "Enjoyed meeting you at Phil's surprise party—would love to talk to your uncle about his sales position at Company X." This will jar their memory of you two weeks from now when they pull your card out of their pocket along with their Pizza Hut receipt and gum wrappers. Then be Detective Diana and get the names and numbers of both the person you met and their contact so that you can personally follow up.

CAREER CENTERS AT COLLEGES AND SCHOOLS

These are free, and it's just plain foolish not to take advantage of them. Many companies come and interview on campus. Even if you've graduated from school, you paid a lot of money to go there, so you can still take advantage of them. Often schools have an alumni job hotline that you can call. Talk to professors and mentors that you admire. In addition to their teaching stints, many of them also do consulting in their field or know others who do.

PROFESSIONAL ORGANIZATIONS

Get involved in a local professional organization or club (e.g., Public Relations Society of America, Society of Professional Engineers, etc.). They often host cool seminars, workshops, and programs in your field, and obviously it will be loaded with people in your industry. Often these organizations offer a membership discount for recent college grads or those professionals under age twenty-five.

CHAMBER OF COMMERCE EVENTS

Many chambers of commerce offer different kinds of functions, but one of the most popular is the Business After Hours event.

These are usually held after work from 5-7 P.M., and while they appear to be happy hours involving business small talk and beanie weenies, these are primo networking opportunities.

CLASSIFIEDS AND WEB SITES

Check the online classifieds section of your local newspaper. Many employers no longer waste time and money on actual newspaper ads because they're looking for computer and Internet savvy people. It's okay to seek out the classifieds, but don't limit yourself to them and don't spend too much time. It's the first place everyone looks, so you'll be competing with a lot of other Jills and Joes. Web sites can be a bit overwhelming, but Yahoo! HotJobs (*www.hotjobs.com*), Monster (*www.monster.com*), and Careerbuilder (*www.careerbuilder.com*) are three good sources to tap. All three sites provide large job databases, career and résumé advice, and networking opportunities, plus you can post your résumé online.

INDUSTRY TRADE SHOWS

A trade show is a convention where different entities in an industry come together to show and compare products, services, and ideas. There are often displays, presentations, receptions, seminars, giveaways, and, of course, a lot of schmoozing. For example, Book Expo America is a huge book publishing event showcasing publishers, books, trends, authors, and retailers, so if you want to establish contacts and possibly land a job in publishing, this is the place to be. Just about every profession has at least one main trade show and often there are more. Be sure to take a lot of your business cards with you and make the most of this industry lovefest.

EMPLOYMENT AGENCIES (HEADHUNTERS)

Look for an agency that specializes in placing jobs in your field. Make sure the agency you choose is stable and reliable and find out if it is a member of the National Association of Personnel Services. Before you sign with any agency, find out who pays the finder's fee—it should be the employer.

OTHER SOURCES OF INFORMATION

Read your industry's leading literature, your community newspaper, and your local business journal. Be in the loop on who's expanding and who's downsizing—obviously, there will be more opportunities with companies that are growing, not those that are shrinking. Sometimes positions are advertised. When I read in my local newspaper that a certain company would be adding 300 jobs in the next four months, I called my friend Shannon who was looking for a job. She immediately contacted them, stayed in touch, got an interview with them when they were ready to hire, and landed a job.

GET A JOB

The Cover Letter

The purpose of the cover letter is to get the interest of the right recipients and convince them that you're just the candidate they've been looking for. It should also highlight or expand upon the information that will follow in the résumé and make the reader *want* to look at your résumé. It's your moment in the spotlight—for a few seconds—so make the most of it.

After the date, the first section of the cover letter should have the recipient's name, title, company's name, and company's address. Make sure you have the correct spelling of the company and employer. Always try to find out the name of the specific person responsible for filling the position. This has more warm fuzzies than "Dear Sir."

The first paragraph should explain why you are writing. Mention what position you are applying for and how you know of it. The second paragraph should explain what qualifies you for the position, what makes you a better candidate than anyone else, and why you would be a good fit for the company. Toot your own horn, but be truthful. Highlight and expand on the strongest points of your résumé. The third paragraph is open, but this is where I like to kiss up. Has the company won any awards, expanded, or had any articles written about them? If so, congratulate them. The fourth and final paragraph should conclude your letter by announcing the next course of action—the one that *you* are going to take. Note a specific date when you'll follow up (and plan to do it).

That said, the cover letter doesn't have to be boring. In fact just the opposite is true. It has to be interesting enough to stand out from the sea of other cover letters. You can be creative and still be professional. I'm not talking pink paper or neon markers or cheesy clip art. But put some punch in that first sentence of your cover letter like I did for the public relations job I mentioned in the beginning of this chapter.

Bottom line: find out what the company and the job is all about, and hone your cover letter so that you look like a natural fit. Don't send out the same general cover letter for volumes of different jobs. Include any specific buzzwords that were used on the posting for the job, and address any requirements listed. Visit Monster.com's résumé center for sample cover letters and visit the library for some great books with lots of sample résumés and cover letters.

The Résumé

The whole point of your résumé is to make the reader think, "Wow! I *must* talk to her!" According to RésuméDoctor (*www.résumé-doctor.com*), a professional résumé consulting service, recruiters spend *less than ten seconds* reviewing a résumé. Which means you have ten seconds to grab their attention and provide a pretty convincing argument as to why they just gotta have you.

In general, a good résumé has the following sections, but adjust yours to best work for you. Consult any résumé-writing Web site or book for additional formatting advice and samples, but remember—it's easiest to read

Cover Letter and Résumé Checklist

✓ Be brief and use clear, concise language.

✓ Keep the cover letter and résumé to one page each.

✓ Use a variety of active verbs. "Managed," "created," "directed," "produced," and "implemented" are great terms.

✓ Use one simple typeface, two at the most. Times, Chicago, and Helvetica are all good choices.

✓ Allow enough white space between lines to be easy on the eyes.

✓ Use 8½ x 11" white or off-white linen paper.

✓ Avoid photos, graphics, and color. (But it is okay to include a small logo for yourself if you have one.)

✓ Edit your résumé for meaning, clarity, grammar, and punctuation. Double check your spelling and use Spell Check.

✓ Solicit critiques by peers, career counselors, or someone "in the know."

✓ If you're sending a résumé via e-mail, send a test to yourself first and check that everything is okay.

a résumé that boldfaces or underlines the heading of each sections, allows ample space between sections, and uses plenty of white space.

PERSONAL DATA

At the top and center of the page, put your name in large type (about 24-point type). Include your mailing address, telephone number(s), e-mail address, and a fax number if you have one. Do not include any references to marital status, age, sex, or religion—legally, an employer cannot ask you for or use any of this information in hiring.

WORK EXPERIENCE

This is where you can brag. Many résumés organize this chronologically by date (starting with the most recent experience), but you can also organize it functionally, selecting important skills relevant to the job for which you are applying. For each job listed, include the title, company, time frame worked, location, and a brief description of your responsibilities and accomplishments.

EDUCATION

If you're just out of college and don't have a lot of relevant experience, this part might come before the work experience section. It should include the school, location of the school, your major/degree, GPA (if a 3.0 or above), and degree year. You might also include any relevant courses, workshops, or seminars that you completed.

SKILLS

Write a line or two highlighting any licenses that you have and any computer, technical, language, or other skills relevant to the position.

HONORS AND ACHIEVEMENTS

This is where you can brag some more. Highlight any awards you've won, honors you've received, or any other impressive feats you've accomplished.

MEMBERSHIPS AND ACTIVITIES

Include any memberships and activities relevant to the position for which you are applying. If you aren't yet affiliated with any pertinent groups, take some time to join one now—before you finalize your résumé. That way, you can honestly list these memberships on your résumé, and, hey, you were meaning to join up anyway, right?

REFERENCES

It's nice to do anything you can to make it easier for a potential employer to hire you. If you have the space, go ahead and include three references and their telephone numbers at the bottom of your résumé. While it's cool to list someone who is a company president or CEO, you're better off to list people who really know you and will talk you up to a potential boss. But hey, if you do know a company president or CEO really well, definitely include them. Better yet, ask *them* for a job. (Courtesy call your references to make sure it's okay to list them *and* so they'll be prepared in case they receive a call.)

Always follow up every résumé that you send out in the manner and on the day that you wrote you would. Be persistent, but not pesky. It is possible that your résumé accidentally got tossed in the trash with a sandwich wrapper (ewwww—gross!), but unless you follow up with a phone call or e-mail, you won't know.

When following up, three things should happen: First, don't leave a voicemail—call 100 times if you have to, but *talk to a person*. (Block your Caller ID if necessary—a restraining order isn't exactly the kind of recognition that you want.) If you get someone's voicemail, hit "0" and ask to be connected directly to your contact. Also, try calling before normal business hours: many managers are in early in the morning before their assistants are there to screen calls. Second, have your pitch rehearsed for when they do answer or it's Game Over—and you've lost. Third, give them your pitch and get an interview set up before you hang up the phone. Be polite, brief, and get to the point quickly. Something like:

> Hello, Mr. Smith, this is Jane Doe. I submitted my résumé to you electronically July 5 for the Account Executive position you advertised in *The Kansas City Star*. I hope you've had a chance to revlew my résumé and I'd like to meet with you to discuss it. When are you available next week?

This polite but assertive approach makes it difficult for a potential employer to refuse you an interview.

The Interview

If you've gotten an interview, you're halfway there! They're interested, they're giving you a chance, and now it's your turn to knock their socks off. Your ability to click with your interviewer (as well as anyone else you meet) is key. They're evaluating you as someone they would—or would not—like to work with.

DO YOUR HOMEWORK
This sounds obvious, but it's amazing how many people don't even know the correct spelling or pronunciation of their target

company—or even the person with whom they're interviewing. Get on the Internet and cruise the company's Web page. Study industry trends. Do enough research to be able to speak knowledgeably in your interview. Have they received any awards? Acquired a new client? Expanded in any way? A nice way to start off an interview is to be smart *and* flatter a potential new boss.

REHEARSE

Practice interviewing with a friend. Videotaping (don't cringe) your practice interview and reviewing it is very helpful. Do you make eye contact? Do you fidget or have any nervous habits? Do you smile easily? Count how many times you say "uh" or "um" and I guarantee you'll make a conscious effort not to do it anymore. Try this little trick I use in presentations. When you feel an "um" or "uh" is about to pop out of your mouth, just close your mouth and say nothing. It might feel awkward, but the silence will sound so much better. Prepare yourself for the kinds of questions an employer might toss out.

DRESS FOR SUCCESS

If you live in a different city than where the job you are applying

Frequently Asked Job Interview Questions

Here are some general but frequently asked questions during a job interview. Of course, it's also a good idea to be prepared for specific questions based on your résumé or about your industry, skills, and training.

✓ Why are you looking for a job/ leaving your current job?

✓ Tell me about yourself.

✓ What are your strengths and weaknesses?

✓ Describe a challenge that you faced and how you handled it.

✓ What do you know about our company?

✓ Why do you want to work for this company?

✓ Why should we hire you?

✓ What accomplishment are you the most proud of?

✓ What motivates you?

for is, you may do an interview over the telephone. But it's more likely that your interview will be face to face, so unless you're applying to be a tattoo artist, the look you're going for is professional, polished, and conservative. Even if you interview on a Friday and the company you're interviewing with endorses Casual Fridays, do *not* dress casually. A navy or black suit (with a skirt that hits no more than an inch above the knee) with a blouse, sheer hose, and sensible heels is always a wise choice. Double-check that you don't have any buttons loose or missing, that everything is clean and ironed and free of cat hair, that your hose doesn't have runs, and that your shoes are polished. Carry just *one* bag, preferably a briefcase or attaché case (stick a small purse inside), and a portfolio if applicable. Leave the backpack at the dorm and the gym bag in the locker where they belong.

BE PREPARED

Take the route to your interview site beforehand, preferably at the same time of day. Allow plenty of time for unforeseen stuff like weather and traffic, and arrive early (but not too early—ten minutes is perfect). Bring a couple of extra copies of your résumé in your attaché case or a "leave behind" handout of samples of your portfolio's best work. Be sure to also take a pad of paper, pen, lipstick, an extra pair of hose, and safety pins. Breath mints are a good idea, but chewing gum is not.

END ON A HIGH NOTE

Your interview will probably end with your interviewer asking if you have any questions. *Always* have three questions in mind, and one shouldn't be, "Which way to the ladies' room?" If you haven't had a chance to discuss this already, ask, "What can I do for your company to make it even more successful?" Don't ask about the money—ask about the *opportunity*. There will be plenty of time to discuss the bling after an offer is made. Also, find out what their timeframe is for making a decision. This will help you gauge when you should check in if you haven't heard back.

FOLLOW THROUGH

Follow up your interview with a thank you. I prefer handwritten or typed snail mail versus e-mail—it shows you made an effort. This is your last chance to seal the deal. Thank the person for taking the time to meet with you and indicate what you learned about the company that would make you a great fit for the position. Reiterate how excited you are at the prospect of working there. Conclude your thank you with what *you'll* do next—name a specific date or time that you'll contact him or her (and plan to do it).

The Offer

Congratulations! Being offered that first real job is a moment you—and your parents—will always remember with pride. Even if you're tempted to yell, "Yes! I'll start Monday!"—don't. Never will you be more in a position to negotiate than when you're offered a job, so be ready to wheel and deal. Get the offer explained in detail and ask for a few days to think it over.

Here are a few of the main things you should ask about when made an offer:

TITLE

This is the most basic information. Also find out the name and title of your immediate supervisor.

SALARY

This is the most important part of the offer for you to consider in your decision, so get clarity on what the base pay is and how often you'll receive a paycheck.

REVIEWS AND PROMOTIONS

Ask if you can have a review in six months and find out when you will be eligible for a raise. Also ask how the promotion process works.

BONUSES

This adds money to your total compensation package. If bonuses are offered, find out if they are tied to your personal perform- ance, the company's performance, or both.

INSURANCE BENEFITS

The most important benefits are health and dental insurance, and most employers also offer life insurance. Be sure to find out the provider, the types of coverage offered, how much your company pays, and how much you will pay in premiums out of your own pocket. Also, it's very important to find out when your health insurance will kick in—you never, *ever* want to be with- out health insurance for any reason.

FINANCIAL BENEFITS

Find out about the company's pension plans, retirement plans, life insurance, and stock options. Be sure to ask when the "vesting" period begins (how long you have to be employed before you're eligible) and how long you need to stay until you're fully vested.

TIME OFF

In general, employers offer one to two weeks of vacation a year with more weeks accrued the longer you're there. Vacation time is often negotiable, so if you are offered less time compared with what you want or have at a current job, ask for more. Also ask about sick days, personal days, and floating company holidays.

PERKS

Parking, reduced gym memberships, tuition reimbursement, movie discounts, free company products, etc., are just some of the perks many companies offer.

START DATE

Find out when your first day on the job will be. If you're currently employed, as a professional courtesy, it's a good idea to give two-weeks notice. Even if you hate your boss, hate your job, and hate your life in general, stick it out for two more weeks. It's unbelievable how small the business world is, and you don't want to burn bridges.

Your employer should send you an official letter stating your offer in writing, but be sure to get *everything* in writing that has been agreed upon and that's important to you. If you're asked to sign a contract, review it thoroughly, or better yet, seek legal advice for it. If nothing else, buy a buddy in law school a drink and ask them to look at it (before they've had that drink, though).

I GOT THE JOB! NOW WHAT?!

Now that you've got the job, you want to make sure that you not only keep it, but that you go gangbusters so you get more opportunities. During a shaky economy, companies will be looking to let their weakest links go, and you want to do everything you can to make sure you're not the charm that gets chucked off the bracelet. It's more important than ever to prove not just how valuable you are, but how *invaluable* you are.

Here's one thing that college didn't prepare you for: there can be a lot of, well, *interesting* characters in the office. People have very different personalities, backgrounds, agendas, and work styles. Maybe Sue gets huffy when her ideas are challenged, or Rick constantly brags about his talent, or John has this annoying habit of clipping his toenails at his desk. You don't have to like everyone, but you do have to learn how to work with them professionally and successfully. Figure out the key people and relationships. Although decisions should be made based on tangible information and logic, they're often based on office politics. It's not fair but it's the way it is, so the sooner you accept it, get over it, and rock despite it, the better off you'll be.

Here are just a few rungs to master on your climb up the corporate ladder:

KEEP A LID ON IT

It's okay to have a personal life, but it's not okay to broadcast every detail of it to your colleagues and especially your boss. So keep the fight with your boyfriend, the latest thing your mother has done to drive you crazy, and what you remember of last weekend's pub crawl to yourself. You don't want to give the impression that your personal problems are so big they're spilling over into your professional life. And don't partake in office gossip, no matter how tempting.

WATCH THE PERSONAL PHONE CALLS, E-MAILS, AND INTERNET BROWSING

Be careful whom you give your office number and email address out to. You don't want that important conversation with your boss interrupted by your best friend Amy's third call today. Remember, companies have every right to read your e-mail, and they do. It's not uncommon for people to be fired not only for the content of their personal e-mails, but also for how much time they spend writing them. My rule of thumb is never to send out an e-mail that you would not want your boss to see (because he just might). Consider opening your own personal e-mail account on sites such as Yahoo! or Hotmail. On the same note, keep your Internet searches relevant to your job. Companies can monitor how much time you spend surfing the net and the sites you visit.

REMEMBER THAT APPEARANCE IS EVERYTHING

From the way you dress to how tidy your office is to whether you're on time for meetings, your boss will notice every detail—especially if it isn't up to snuff. Dress for success and to impress (see chapter 8 for how to pull together a professional wardrobe). Get face time in with your boss—before she can see you as a key member of her team, she has to just see you, period. Be neat. Keep your work area tidy and organized so that you can find whatever you—or anyone else—might need pronto. You'd hate to have your boss standing over you as you dig through your pile o' crap looking for that important report. Keep in mind that people tend to associate neatness with a good work ethic.

FAKE IT SO YOU CAN MAKE IT

Give the impression that you're a workaholic and a perfectionist whether or not you really are. Get in before your boss and leave afterward. Always look like you're productive, even if you're really thinking about your date with that cute guy from the gym.

EXCEED EXPECTATIONS

Complete projects thoroughly, neatly, and *before* their deadlines. Go above and beyond what you are asked for. If your boss wants five ideas, give ten. If he asks for a report by Friday, give it to him Thursday.

Desk Dos and Don'ts

Do: A framed picture of your family, nephew, or even your cat (but skip the homemade "paw-painted" frame that reads My Baby).

Don't: A framed picture of you and your girlfriends trashed on your Booze Cruise in Mexico.

Do: A coffee mug that displays an interest, hobby, or vocation, like "Teachers Have Class" or "Go Mizzou!"

Don't: A coffee mug that reads, "110% Goth." Ditto the *South Park* cup (unless you work for Comedy Central).

Do: An emergency emery board in the drawer of your desk.

Don't: A manicure set and enough nail polish to paint the Sistine Chapel.

Do: A local and national newspaper, the business journal, and relevant trade publications.

Don't: A half-done crossword puzzle, your iPod, or the latest issue of *Glamour* magazine.

MAKE YOURSELF PART OF THE SOLUTION

Your boss wants answers, not problems. So if there's a crisis, don't go to him in a tizzy until you can calmly offer your well-thought-out solutions. The thing that makes you least valuable to your boss is making your problems become your boss's problems. But don't be afraid to ask for help if you're in over your head. Your boss most likely didn't get where he is without having succeeded in the job that you're doing now. After all, dropping the ball on a project is much worse than asking for help.

WATCH YOUR SPENDING

Even if you don't work in the accounting department, it pays to suggest ways to cut costs to the higher-ups. Even if it's just a few bucks—say sending something UPS Ground instead of FedEx overnight or using a black-and-white copier instead of a color copier for in-house memos—you'll be thought of as smart.

SPEAK UP

Inside or outside of the office, no one appreciates a motormouth with nothing to say who wastes everyone's time saying it. But if you don't speak up, you may come across as bored, lazy, or just not very bright. Have confidence in yourself and your ideas. Don't start off with, "Maybe this isn't a good idea, but . . . ." You want to set colleagues up to cheer, not jeer. Make copies of relevant material or articles that support your ideas and hand them out to everyone.

BE MISS CONGENIALITY

You should have learned how to work and play well with others in kindergarten, but if you haven't, now's the time to share your crayons. Giving other people credit for their work is one of the easiest ways to be liked, plus they'll be more eager to help you again. Even if you don't agree with a particular idea, offer constructive feedback instead of criticism. Whether it's praising a great idea in a brainstorming session or rooting on your colleagues at the company softball game, being part of the team is important.

BE SOCIAL—BUT NOT TOO SOCIAL

Whether it's a company dinner or an unofficial happy hour after work, don't drink too much. It's okay to let your hair down in front of your friends; it's never okay to booze it up in front of your boss or colleagues. Nurse one cocktail, but then stick to soda or water for the rest of the evening. You'll be better off in the morning for so many reasons. And speaking of being social, remember that the office is not your personal dating pool. In fact, some company policies strictly forbid office romances.

MASTER THE ART OF SMALL TALK

There will be times when you'll be alone with your superiors—rides in the elevator, a few minutes before a meeting, a business lunch—and you want to use those times to your advantage. Avoid controversial or too-personal topics such as politics, religion, and sex. Keep it polite and general. Ask him how his new puppy is, how his daughter's ballet recital went, or if he enjoyed his golf game this weekend. It doesn't have to be too intellectual—you just want to make contact. You want your boss to be comfortable in your presence and see you as an ally.

BETTER YOURSELF

Become an expert at something. Whether it's Internet research, spotting industry trends, or trimming budgets, find that thing you do well—and do it. Keep your skills current to keep yourself valuable to the company. Take a course, read a book, attend a lecture, master the newest update of your computer, or take a time management course. If you want to take a college course, check with your company's HR department to see if they'll pay the tuition (many do).

READ RELEVANT PUBLICATIONS

Whether it's the newspaper, business journals, or trade publications, know what's happening in the world and your little piece of it. Cut out interesting articles and file them away for later use. Or better yet, share photocopies with coworkers who might also be interested.

ADOPT A MENTOR

Finding a professional that you admire and who is older, wiser, and more experienced can be invaluable. A mentor can take you under his or her wing and provide advice, support, and even opportunities. Maybe it's a former college professor, a family friend, or someone in the industry. Ask them for a monthly lunch date (and be sure to pick up the tab). They'll be flattered you asked.

Asking for a (Gulp!) Raise

In addition to adopting the above-mentioned tips, the best way to get promoted is to take on responsibilities for the position that you want. From your boss's point of view, it will seem like a natural transition to promote you to the job if you're already doing it.

Timing is everything. If you've recently been praised for a succession of projects, it may be a good time to ask for a raise. After your company has just gone through its third round of layoffs is not. You'll have to prove a case for yourself, so keep an ongoing "job diary" of your biggest coups. Most companies provide their employees with a performance review once a year, and this is often a good time to ask for a raise or promotion.

Even if you're Employee of the Year, there are other issues to consider when asking for a raise. What are the current business climate factors? What is the company's current financial state? How is your department's performance and your individual performance? How is the economy overall? Research the market range for your job in your geographical area and be sure to know what you're worth before you ask for more.

Even when the economy is tough, you can still do a little negotiating—and it doesn't always mean money. If you know a raise just isn't possible, ask your boss for some extra time off, often called "comp time." If you've been putting in a lot of overtime, you're in a particularly good position to ask him to pony up. You'll be seen as a loyal employee and team player for understanding that the company is not in a position to give you more moolah at this time.

Besides making a fabulous cuppa joe in the morning and sharpening pencils to a needle's point, what talents and capabilities do you bring to the workplace?

....

....

....

....

....

What was your dream job when you were twelve? What elements of that job still appeal to you? What elements don't?

....

....

....

....

....

If you had to decide this minute, what would you want to do with the rest of your life?

....

....

....

....

....

What are your values, wants, goals, and preferences in a job? What would make it fulfilling for you?

....

....

....

....

....

What are your skills and talents? Strengths and weaknesses?

....

....

....

....

....

TO DO! During the job hunt you will . . .

Stay in touch with your contacts.
....

....

....

....

....

Cover letter keepers. What accomplishment statements sell you?

I created a new system to track all company payments.

....

....

....

CHEAT SHEET! Respond to job interview questions on page 22.

....

....

....

....

TO DO! After you get the job . . .

Send thank-you notes to anyone who helped along the way.

Shop for new office-worthy wardrobe essentials.

....

....

....

....

....

2

Dollars
and Sense

A budget with your money is
just like going on a diet with
your weight . . . It's not about
making more, it's about keeping
more of what you already
make.

—SUZE ORMAN

WHEN I WAS SIX YEARS OLD, I GOT A WEEKLY ALLOWANCE OF 75¢. I MANAGED MY MONEY VIA THE TUPPERWARE Method: I had three separate Tupperware bowls, one labeled "Spending," one labeled "Church and Charity," and one labeled "Savings." Each week, I'd put a quarter in each bowl. I didn't know exactly what I was saving up for with my "Savings" dish, but I knew that someday I'd be glad I was squirreling money away.

A few months later I was at the local flea market when I spied a huge dollhouse—complete with furniture—on sale for $2. I had to think it over carefully. After all, that was eight weeks' worth of savings! But, I was tired of my Barbie's makeshift penthouse on top of my parents' old Victrola, so I took the plunge. Barbie and I both enjoyed her home for several years before I sold it for $5; I guess you could say it was my first real-estate purchasing experience.

This is a pretty simplistic example of money management, but the basic concept still applies: if you make a budget, stick to it, and save accordingly, you can have things that you want someday.

"BUDGET" IS NOT A FOUR-LETTER WORD

If you're really lucky, you've either got a big trust fund or a six-figure income. But if you're like the remaining 99 percent of us, you're probably working a lot of long hours not only to pay your dues, but just to try and pay your bills. Well, take comfort in the fact that most of us have been there and it won't always be that way. Be patient, and know that if you continue to work hard, you'll eventually have more buying power.

Once you have a job and know what your income will be, the first thing to do is make a budget to help you plan accordingly. Before you roll your eyes and ask for a shot of tequila, think of a budget as a tool for helping you achieve your financial goals and dreams, not a penny-pinching sacrifice that doesn't let you have any fun. It's like going on a diet versus eating healthy: a diet is negative, restrictive, and makes you miserable; eating healthy is positive, permits you to indulge now and then and still achieve your goals, and allows you to enjoy life.

Money helps you reach your goals in life, but until you know where that money goes, you can't make conscious decisions to save for the things you want. Think about what your financial goals are. Do you want to buy a car? A house? Take a vacation to the Bahamas and sip mai tais while a cute cabana boy rubs suntan oil on your back? Try breaking down each goal into short term (one year or less), medium-term (one to three years), and long-term (five years or more) time frames.

Separate the needs from the wants—and be honest. Do you

really *need* to have your nails filed at the salon every two weeks or *need* that $5 espresso every morning? (Although, I'm sure many a non-morning person would declare a jolt of java a necessity.) It's all about prioritizing and give and take. If you don't want to give up the salon manicure or commercialized coffee, can you cut back on the number of dinners out? If you stick with a realistic, effective budget long enough, the rewards will keep you *wanting* to budget.

Try this little exercise (humor me) and challenge yourself: Carry a small notepad with you and keep track of every cent you spend for just two weeks. The $1 Snickers from the vending machine at work, the (four) newest shades of perfect lip gloss, the latest romance novel by the checkout counter—you'll be surprised how much these trifling purchases add up to.

A good software program like Quicken can help you take care of your basic financial transactions, but you can also create and track a budget just by inserting a table into a Word program or sketching one out with pen and paper. The next page shows a sample budget with a basic list of things to consider—use it to get started. Personalize it with your particular wants and needs. Make twelve copies of your sheet (one for each month) and put them in a folder.

At the beginning of the month, fill in the dollar amounts for the Monthly Estimated Budget Columns that apply to you. As you actually purchase the items or services during the month, write down the dollar amount in the Monthly Actual Budget. Then, at the end of the month, calculate the difference between your estimated and actual amounts, putting a "+" in front of the difference if you spent less than you estimated and a "-" in front of the difference if you spent more than you estimated.

INCOME AND EXPENSES

	ESTIMATED	ACTUAL	DIFFERENCE
INCOME			
Wages paid			
Bonuses			
Interest earned			
Misc. income			
Total Income			
EXPENSES			
Charity			
Clothing			
Club memberships			
Emergency			
Entertainment			
Concerts			
Dinners/drinks out			
Hobbies			
Movies			
Sports			
Other			
Gifts			
Groceries			
Health and beauty			
Services			
Toiletries			
Home maintenance			
Household items			
Laundry/dry cleaning			
Insurance			
Car			
Health			
Life			
Renter's			
Miscellaneous			
Pets			
Rent/mortgage			
Savings/investments			
Student loans			
Taxes			
Transportation			
Car payment			
Gasoline			
Maintenance/repair			
Parking			
Public			
Tolls			
Utilities			
Cable (basic)			
Electricity			
Gas			
Phone/cell phone			
Water			
Total Budget			

The purpose of the sample budget isn't to bum you out or dissuade you from ever buying a Fendi bag. It's just to bring to your attention to where your money goes. Sometimes something isn't evident until you see it in writing.

Some months it will be easier than others to meet your budget, and it's not important to follow it dollar-for-dollar. But recording your spending will get you in the habit of setting and meeting a budget. You might want to take a look at your spending habits after three, six, or twelve months to see where you need to buckle down or to pat yourself on the back. If you come in ahead of your budget in one area, resist the temptation to splurge in another. Instead, take that unexpected extra money and save it or, better yet, invest it.

Additionally, keeping your checkbook balanced and up-to-date will help you manage your money. It also verifies that your records match the bank's, and while your bank processes thousands of transactions successfully every day, mistakes do happen, and you'd rather they didn't happen to you.

GIVE ME SOME CREDIT!

Credit cards are convenient for doing things like renting cars, reserving hotel rooms, purchasing airline tickets, and buying anything over the Internet. They're also great if you're out of town and your car breaks down or you have some other unexpected situation come up where you'll need to pay a big sum pronto: an out-of-town check would likely be unaccepted and it's doubtful you'd have that much cash. When used properly, a credit card is a much-appreciated tool; when used improperly, a credit card can be your worst nightmare.

You do need one credit card, but probably no more than that. And use that one sparingly. Resist the temptation to use credit cards to buy what you want but can't afford. Pay with cash when you can because it makes the purchase immediate and real, and you might even think twice about whether you really need it at all. "Just Say No" when stores offer you a 10 percent discount on your purchase that day if you open an account. A 10 percent savings isn't a savings if you develop a habit of going back to all of those stores and spending money on things you don't really need.

Consider keeping a running tab on what you've used your credit card for during the month so you're not surprised when the bill arrives. And *really* watch your credit card use during the month of December. Paying with cash for gifts, decorations, wrapping paper, and new outfits for all of your holiday soirees will make your January statement much kinder.

If your credit card has an annual fee, call and ask the company to waive it and they probably will. If they don't, close out that account and get a card with no annual fee. Always pay off your credit card in full each month to avoid paying any interest *and* so that you don't carry debt over to the next month. If you don't think you can afford to pay it off each month, what you really can't afford is all the stuff you're charging to your credit card. Scale back somewhere. If after a year you're doing well making your payments each month, ask your credit card company to raise your credit limit.

Thanks to credit cards, it's not hard to establish credit. Just make sure you're establishing the kind of credit history that you want. Your credit history is a record of everything related to any credit you've ever had or applied for. It includes the 411 of where you've worked and how you pay your bills. It's important to be aware of your credit history because it affects many of the things you want to do in life. You don't want to wait until you're ready to buy a car or a home and have to get a credit report done and it's not good. You can get a copy of your credit report from Trans Union Credit Information Services (*www.transunion.com*), Experian (*www.experian.com*), or Equifax Credit Services (*www.equifax.com*).

STAY OUT OF THE DEBT NET

The best way to handle debt is not to get in it in the first place. But if you do, act fast before it snowballs on you. The very first thing you need to do is stop spending *now*. Buy only the very, very basics you need to live: food, water, and shelter. (And insurance, of course. As I wrote in chapter 1 and as you'll see me write again in chapter 10, never, *ever* go without insurance.) If you don't want to stop spending money, you need to start making more, but this probably requires quite a jump in income by either switching jobs or getting a promotion. A great solution if it happens, but don't count on it as your ticket out.

If you carry over a balance from month to month, chill out on using your credit card altogether until you get things under control. Put it away, or if you're really tempted to use it, cut it up. Believe me, you can always get another one.

Take a good look at what you owe and to whom you owe it. Contact creditors and let them know you're aware of your debt and are trying to pay it off. See if they'll put together a payment plan with you—most of them will if you are honest and upfront about your problem and act in good faith. Once you've worked out a plan, stick to it—you can't afford any more goofs.

Don't ignore any bills. "Make even a small payment on your bill to keep from damaging your credit," advises Mark Hassenflu, vice president of Stern Brothers & Co. and manager of private client investments, who advises individuals on their financial planning needs. "Your credit report reflects the number of accounts that have been turned over to a collection agency. Once your bill has even been turned over to an agency, it could hurt your credit rating."

Think about other (legal!) sources to get the money you need to pay off your debts. As hard as it might be, can you suck it up and ask your parents for help and put together a plan for how you'll pay them back? Can you downsize or even sell your car? Do you have anything else—stereo equipment, clothes, books, knickknacks—that you can sell to second-hand stores or on eBay? Can you take a second job waiting tables, babysitting, or working retail in the evenings and on weekends, even if it's for minimum wage?

If you really think you're in trouble, contact Debtors Anonymous. They will put you in touch with counselors who specialize in personal financial recovery, and some of them work for nonprofit organizations so you can obtain their services for free or a very small fee. Contact your Better Business Bureau and check them out.

If all else fails—and I mean really fails—you can file for personal bankruptcy. This is something you absolutely want to avoid at all costs. Declaring personal bankruptcy will cost a few hundred dollars in legal fees and will stain your credit record for *ten years*. But it will all be over, and you can start clean.

SAVING FOR A RAINY DAY OR A VACATION OR A CAR OR A HOUSE OR . . .

Even if you have some money to invest, you've probably put off doing so, because, well, it's kinda boring. Honestly, it's not as much fun as happy hour with your gal pals. But it's not too agonizing, and you'll probably sleep better at night once you just do it.

Once you're able to put some money away, a savings account is the first place it should go. Think of saving as spending money on your future. A savings account is also a great emergency fund should an unexpected expense arise and you need to get money immediately (see chapter 10). Financial experts recommend keeping three to six months' salary in your emergency fund. (And no, an end-of-season Ann Taylor pantsuit doesn't qualify as an emergency.)

After you've established your emergency savings fund, you're meeting your budget, and your debt is under control, you're ready to turn your saving into *investing*. Savings accounts are nice and safe, but they earn little interest. Saving your money is great but investing it is even better. A

penny saved is a penny earned, but a penny invested is, well, a lot more pennies! You've worked hard for your money, and now you can make your money work for you.

The key to successful investing is to start early and continue investing regularly at a slow and steady pace. Think about it—if get-rich-quick schemes really worked, don't you think everyone would get rich pretty quickly? Thinking small now will pay off big later. Let's say you save just $10 a week for a year—and anyone should be able to do that pretty painlessly (see the end of this chapter for some suggested ideas). That's a savings of $520 a year, and a savings of $2,600 in five years.

But let's take it a step further. Let's say you *invested* that $10 at a simple interest rate of 5 percent. You'd have $546 instead of $520 a year, and $2,730 instead of $2,600 in five years. All for doing nothing more than brown-bagging it to lunch now and then and letting your money sit in an account. See how easy that is?

When you start investing, you might want to find a broker or financial planner to help. A good place to start is with someone your family trusts and uses. Regardless of whether or not you choose to use a broker or financial planner, here are some common types of investment terms defined:

CHECKING ACCOUNT

This keeps your money and allows you to write checks from it instead of paying cash. Most accounts pay no or minimal interest, but they do have fees and conditions (e.g., you have to keep a minimum balance or you'll be charged). Check around (no pun intended). Keep track of your money or you risk bouncing checks—and paying a penalty for every check that is bounced.

Your checking account will probably also come with an ATM (automatic teller machine) card that lets you withdraw money from your account, check your account balance, or transfer money between your checking and savings accounts at an ATM when you enter your PIN (personal identification number). The best thing about ATMs is that they are virtually everywhere and open 24-7, but you can get into trouble if you don't exercise a little restraint. If you don't use your own bank's ATM, you'll probably be charged a fee (usually between $1.50 and $5.00) for every transaction that you make. So if you withdraw money once a week and are charged $3 each time, that's $156 a year in unnecessary charges!

SAVINGS ACCOUNT

A savings account is like a checking account except that all banks pay interest on savings accounts. Not a lot, but something. The average savings account earns about 2 percent interest. You have to keep your balance above a minimum and you may have to keep it active for a specified time period. This is a great venue for an emergency fund.

MONEY MARKET ACCOUNT

This is considered a type of savings account and generally pays a bit more interest than a regular savings account. You can write a minimum number of checks (usually three) each month.

CDS

I'm talking certificates of deposits, not compact discs. With a CD, you deposit money for a specified amount of time, usually anywhere from three months to a number of years; the longer your CD, the higher your interest rate. CDs earn more interest than savings accounts and money market accounts, but there's a penalty if you need to get your money out before the specified time. If you have some extra money that you will not need soon, think about CDs.

MUTUAL FUNDS

These are investments that pool the money of several people and place it into stocks, bonds, and other holdings. The money is managed by a portfolio manager who finds the best places to invest the money. Since a lot of people go into it together, you don't have to have a lot of money to get started.

BONDS

A bond is simply an "IOU." You lend money to a bond issuer (the government, municipalities, and companies, to name a few) for a fixed period of time at a set interest rate so that the bond issuer can grow. Bonds are a credit risk because the issuer could default, and they're also an interest-rate risk.

STOCKS

Stock is ownership in a company. Stocks change in price minute to minute, and you will pay a commission to buy or sell. If you have no experience in this area, it's best to look for someone to teach you how the market works and how you can hopefully make money in it. If you have any friends in finance, talk to them, or ask your parents or someone else close to you who is financially responsible to recommend someone.

RETIREMENT?! BUT I'M JUST GETTING STARTED!

Although retirement seems like a long way off—and it is—it's a good idea to start saving for it now. Many companies offer a 401k plan, and this is definitely something you want to take advantage of. A 401k is a type of retirement savings plan that allows employees to contribute a portion of their paychecks to a company-sponsored investment plan with pre-tax dollars.

In addition to the fact that they're flexible and tax-free, 401ks are great because an employer will often match your savings. Not all companies match, but many do. Always contribute the maximum amount allowed into your 401k (most companies will allow you to change this amount during certain periods of the year). The contributions are taken out of your paycheck so you'll never even miss the money. You can't get to the money until you retire, but you can take it with you if you leave a company and roll it into another account.

The amount of the match varies from company to company, but the most typical match is that for every dollar an employee contributes from their paycheck (up to 4 percent), the employer will throw in 50¢. If you're really lucky, your employer will match your contribution dollar for dollar up to a certain percentage. Either way, you don't have to be a financial guru to know that's a great deal!

Roth IRAs are a relatively new retirement plan and a great way for you to contribute to your retirement fund and save on your taxes if you qualify. A Roth IRA is an individual retirement account in which funds placed into the account are non-deductible. For the maximum contribution, the limits are $95,000 for single individuals and $150,000 for married individuals filing joint returns. The amount you can contribute is reduced gradually and then completely eliminated when your modified adjusted gross income exceeds $110,000 (single) or $160,000 (married and filing jointly).

If they are held for more than five years, all funds withdrawn are received tax-free. Many financial experts agree that Roth IRAs are better than traditional IRAs for a lot of reasons. First, your contribution is after-tax money. Second, when you take the money out, it is not considered taxable income. Finally, you can get your money out without penalty anytime after age fifty-nine-and-a-half, but unlike traditional IRAs, you're not required to take the money out when you reach seventy-and-a-half.

A TAXING SUBJECT

The old saying is true—the only two things in life that are certain are death and taxes. The thought of either one is pretty unpleasant for most of us.

The first time you ever got a paycheck, you were probably shocked to see just how much of it went to Uncle Sam. Social Security taxes, Medicaid taxes, federal taxes, state taxes, sometimes even city taxes. But as much as you dislike paying taxes, if you don't pay them, you could end up with some-

thing you'd dislike even more—an IRS agent knocking on your door to find out why you haven't paid up. And then you could be in Big Trouble. Yikes!

Even though you have to pay taxes, there is a (legal) way to reduce the amount of taxes you have to pay: by reducing your amount of taxable income and then using all of the deductions that apply to you. Your taxable income is simply the amount of income for which you are taxed. Your salary (minus your 401k money), bonuses, tips, and interest earned on savings and checking accounts all qualify as taxable income. To make less of your income taxable, you can put it into accounts where it won't be taxed (called tax-sheltered accounts) such as certain retirement accounts.

Deductions are legal, just as long as you only use the ones that apply to you. So, you can't deduct moving expenses if you didn't really move. Most young people have a pretty simple financial situation and take a standard deduction as opposed to an itemized deduction. A standard deduction is a lump-sum amount set by the IRS of allowed deductions that you can subtract from your total taxable income.

If your financial situation is pretty straightforward, you can hire a tax preparer to do your taxes for you. The customary fee is about $100 for a basic tax return. Or, you can prepare your tax return yourself with the help of a software program, book, or Web site. Doing your own taxes will not only save you money, but it will also help you better understand your personal financial situation.

LITTLE WAYS
TO SAVE A LOT

It's very easy to spend just a little money here and there, but over time it adds up—a cup of Starbucks kona each morning, a *People* magazine each week, a pair of earrings with each new outfit. The upcoming chapters offer more in-depth tips as they apply to each chapter's topic, but here are some simple ways you can save a lot just by saving a little:

ENTERTAINMENT

* Use the library, which often gets the latest books in. If you absolutely can't wait, split the cost with a friend who also wants to read the book. You can also rent movies and CDs.

* Keep your TV to basic cable.

* If you find yourself buying the same magazine each month at the checkout counter, get a subscription. You will save a lot more with a yearly subscription versus buying each issue individually. If a friend subscribes to another magazine you like, switch magazines when you're both through.

* Buy season passes for activities that you do frequently. Often this is cheaper than buying individual tickets.

* Rent videos with friends instead of going to the movie theater. It costs the same for ten friends to watch one video as it does for one, plus you have the comfort of hanging out at home.

* Think carefully before spending big bucks on sporting events and concerts. Often it's as much or more fun to watch the event in the comfort of your own place and invite friends over. Plus, you'll get a great seat, good commentary, and pay much less for better food and drink.

✳ Buy soda, juice, water, and beer in multipacks. Keep a
case of soda in your office and stick one or two in the
kitchen fridge if there is one; if not, there's probably an
ice machine. Think about the can of Dr. Pepper you buy
each day at work out of the vending machine. It probably
costs about 60¢. But a 24-pack costs around $5, or about
20¢ a can. So, if you took a can of soda to work each day,
that's a savings of $2 per business week and $104 a year!

✳ To save on takeout, keep a
few frozen entrees in the
freezer at home on hand for
when you're starving and
want something quick. It's as
fast as the drive-through but
cheaper and better for you.

✳ Pack a lunch. You probably
haven't done this since
grade school. Even if you
buy the good smoked turkey
and Provolone cheese at the
grocery store deli and add
some avocado to it, you'll save a lot more than if you
bought a sandwich each day. If you need a little crunch
to go with it, buy a large bag of chips and take a handful
in a sandwich bag each day.

Recommended Reading

If you want to learn more about personal finance, two great books to
check out are *The Complete Idiot's
Guide to Personal Finance In Your
20s and 30s* by Sarah Young
Fisher, Susan Shelly, and Grace W.
Weinstein; and Personal *Finance for
Dummies* by Eric Tyson. Both are
user-friendly guides for those just
beginning personal finance.

✳ If you must indulge your sweet tooth, buy a bag of "fun
size" candy bars and stash a few here and there. Your
wallet—and your waist—will thank you.

✳ Eat breakfast at home, and that doesn't even mean you
have to cook or eat a lot. A bowl of cereal, a glass of
orange juice, a cup of yogurt, or a piece of fruit. Almost
anything you eat will be cheaper and healthier than
something you grab elsewhere. Plus, this will help stave
off the mid-morning munchies when you're tempted to
drop some change in the vending machine for a non-
nutritional snack.

RESTAURANTS

✳ Forgo the drinks (and hors d'oeuvres) at restaurants and have friends over for a cocktail at home before you leave. Many restaurants charge $8 or more for a cocktail or glass of wine. The same goes for coffee, so cap off the night with a cup of decaf at home.

✳ Try restaurants that offer meatless dishes, which will be less expensive. That's why Mexican and Italian restaurants are traditionally less expensive than surf 'n' turf.

✳ Skip the sides if they're not included. The main dish may seem reasonable, but by the time you add on a salad for $3 and some garlic bread for $2, it gets pretty expensive pretty quickly.

✳ "Special" doesn't refer to a reduced price. In fact, it usually means it's something not ordinarily served, so it's often a bit more expensive. Sometimes waiters "forget" to tell you the price of the mouth-watering special they've just recited, so always ask.

✳ Fast food doesn't always mean good food. Yes, it's convenient and will do in a pinch. But don't make a habit of routinely dropping $5 or $6 for a mediocre and forgettable meal.

✳ Get together with friends at someone's apartment and have each person bring a course of the meal. If the word "potluck" doesn't strike your fancy, call it a "progressive dinner."

✳ If there's a new restaurant you've been dying to try, go at lunch instead. The menu items are usually the same but the portions are sometimes smaller and the price is lower.

TRANSPORTATION

✳ Ride a bicycle or walk if it's doable. Invest in good walking shoes and drop the gym membership.

✳ Use public transportation if it's available, or carpool.

* Pay at the pump. This way you'll only buy gas and avoid any overpriced impulse buys at the counter.

* Look for cheap parking. A parking lot a little farther away might be less expensive—just make sure it's safe and well-lit.

TRAVELING

* When vacationing, use discount coupons for hotels, car rentals, and restaurants. These coupons are available on Web sites, your Sunday newspaper, the telephone book, magazines, etc., so look for them.

* Take some time and use the Internet to find the least expensive airline seats, hotels, and car rentals. Cheaptickets.com, Expedia.com, Orbitz.com, and Priceline.com are some to check.

* Think about going in the off-season when prices will be lower.

* Wait until the last minute. If you can be flexible about when and where you'll travel, you might get a great deal because the venue is desperate to fill a space. I did this once for a cruise and got a large, fabulous ocean-view cabin for $300 less than what other people had paid in advance for a tiny, windowless cabin.

BANKING

* As I mentioned previously, use your own bank's ATMs to avoid a fee.

* Have a small amount of money automatically deducted from each paycheck and deposited directly into your savings account. You'll never miss it.

* Pay bills online or set up monthly withdrawals from your checking account. There's no postage or late fees if you're on an automatic plan. Do check yourself that bills have been paid: online banking is quite convenient, but making sure your bills are paid is still *your* responsibility, not the bank's.

UTILITIES

✳ In warm weather, dress cooler and keep your air conditioner at 78°F; set your thermostat to automatically cut the air back during the day while you're at work. Or, avoid using it as much as possible and use ceiling fans or floor fans. Close shades or curtains on sunny windows.

✳ In cold weather, dress warmer and keep your heater at 68°F; set your thermostat to automatically cut the heat back during the day while you're at work. Keep the shades on your windows that get sun open during the day.

✳ Look into prepaid phone cards which might give you cheaper long distance rates.

✳ Make sure you aren't paying for any extra phone services. Three-way calling, call-forwarding, and call-waiting can add $10 a month even when they're a part of your plan.

✳ Periodically call your long distance carrier and then call two competitors to make sure you're still getting the best deal.

✳ If you don't have a self-defrosting freezer (and most older apartments have older appliances that aren't), defrost it at least twice a year.

✳ If you have a fireplace, keep the chimney flues closed except when the fireplace is in use.

✳ Conserve hot water by not letting it continuously run while shaving, bathing, washing your hands, or doing dishes.

✳ It's actually more efficient to use your dishwasher than to wash dishes by hand, but only if you have a full load. Skip the dry cycle and open the door after the final rinse to let everything air dry.

✳ Keep the filters on all heating and cooling units clean.

✳ Use low-flow shower heads.

✳ Use the lowest watt bulbs that will work.

MISCELLANEOUS

✳ Use coupons only for those items you already buy, not to try something new. If there is a particular food product or toiletry that you just love, go to the product's Web site and see if you can download a coupon for it.

✳ Rebates aren't always well advertised. Check the manufacturer's *and* the store's Web sites.

✳ Avoid late fees on everything from your rent to your bills to your library books and videos. Often you only have to be one day late to be hit with a late fee.

✳ Skip the one-hour photo development. C'mon, you can wait—it'll just give you something to look forward to for a few days.

✳ If you absolutely love to shop, go window-shopping. Leave your credit cards, ATM card, checkbook, and cash at home. You'll get the thrill of discovering wonderful, new things without spending any money.

✳ Before you toss an expired gift certificate, check with the venue first. Many will still honor it if you ask, and a growing number of states are outlawing expiration dates on certain types of gift certificates.

✳ Pay with bills instead of coins, and put the change you receive back into a jar at home. At the end of each month, put this change into savings or invest it.

What items, not amounts, go into your "spending bowl"?

....

....

....

Church and charity bowl?

....

....

....

Savings bowl?

....

....

....

What are your short-term financial goals? (Remember: these should be met in 1 year or less.)

....

....

....

Medium-term (1 to 3 years) financial goals?

....

....

....

Long-term (5 years or more) financial goals?

....

....

....

What daily or weekly expenses—big or small—can you cut back on?

....

....

....

CHEAT SHEET! Right now, what's in your . . .

Checking account?

....

Savings account?

....

Money market account?

....

Stocks? Bonds?

....

401(k)?

....

TO DO! Here are your happy hour, deal meal, cheapo date ideas . . .

....

....

....

....

....

....

3

Finding a Place to Call Home

There's no place like home.

—DOROTHY,
THE WIZARD OF OZ

I REMEMBER WATCHING MY PARENTS DRIVE AWAY AFTER MOVING ME INTO MY FIRST APARTMENT. I'D JUST GRADUATED from college and taken my first real job in a big city four hours from my small hometown. My apartment was about the size of the crate I'd hauled my stuff in, had carpet older than I was, and appliances even older than that. But it was all mine. I was proud, excited, and yes, a little nervous about living completely on my own in a new city. Where would I go when (when, not if—I do live in the Midwest) there was a tornado? What if one of the appliances in my apartment broke? What if I slipped in the shower and knocked myself out and (egad!) who would be the one to find me like that?

Okay, perhaps the last scenario is a bit drama queenish even for me, but odd thoughts creep into your mind the first night you're alone in your new place. As it turned out, the laundry facilities in the basement of the apartment complex proved to be good shelter during a tornado, and I got to be on a first-name basis with the maintenance man in my building. My single girl-friends and I developed an informal "check-in" system with each other during bad weather, after dates, or just if we hadn't heard from one another in a few days to make sure we were all alive and well.

RENT OR 'RENTS?

Now that you have a job, know your income, and have made a budget, you can figure out where you want to live. Since the majority of people rent an apartment before they buy a house, this chapter is written with that in mind, but some of the information will still apply to house hunters. (And if you are buying a house, congratulations!)

As a rule of thumb, it's a good idea not to spend more than 25 percent of your monthly gross income (your income before taxes and other deductions) on your rent. So to give you a few guidelines, if you make $20,000 a year, that's $417 a month in rent; $25,000 is $521 a month in rent; $30,000 is $625 a month in rent; and $35,000 is $729 a month in rent.

If you have the option (and the offer), it makes a lot of sense (and will save you a lot of cents) to live at home or with an older sibling, family friend, etc., for just a few months so you can build a nest egg. Even if you offer to pay some living expenses, you'll still be coming out ahead. Better yet, offer some services. Run errands, mow the lawn, do the grocery shopping, help clean, or drive a younger sibling to soccer practice.

Even if your living arrangement is with family or friends, put it in writing—how long the arrangement is for, what you'll contribute, what the agreed-upon rules are. The key to a compatible—and hopefully enjoyable—coexistence is to set up guide-lines and boundaries in advance so that everyone involved has the same set of expectations.

If you do move back home, don't feel bad. You're not alone. According to the most recent Current Population Survey conducted by the U.S. Census Bureau in March 2002, 46 percent of women age 18–24 and 8.3 percent of women age 25–34 lived at home. The high cost of housing, increased age of first marriages, and a tough economy are just some of the reasons living with Mom and Pop is a popular option. Plus, if you have a job and are living rent-free or nearly rent-free, you're in a terrific position to save some money and get ahead.

ROOMIE, OH ROOMIE, WHEREFORE ART THOU, ROOMIE?

The next best option to moving in with family or friends is to get a roommate. Mi casa es su casa. It costs just as much to heat an apartment for one person as it does for two, and often times having a roommate can save you as much as a few hundred dollars a month. In addition to the financial perks, a room-mate can be great company and make you feel safer if you're uncom-

fortable living solo. You can also rent a house with three or four other roomies and have the advantages of a yard, garage, and more space.

Do think carefully about whom you want for a roommate. Living with someone is very different than hanging out with her from time to time. Your best friend may be the most fun person to shop with, but if she's not good about paying her share of the rent, it might ruin your friendship *and* your credit. Trust your instincts: If you have a gut feeling that it's not going to work out, it's probably not going to work out.

Whether it's someone you've known your whole life, an acquaintance from work, or someone you've just met through a roommate placement agency, don't be afraid to ask your potential roomie a lot of questions or to chat with people who know her. Tensions tend to arise when things haven't been discussed, so to avoid a Fourth of July fireworks display, here are some things to ask yourself and potential roommates when considering setting up camp together:

MOOLAH

✓ How much will each person contribute for the deposit?

✓ How will you handle shared expenses like rent, food, utilities, and phone bills?

✓ Will one person write the check and be reimbursed by the other, or will you both write checks?

✓ Can you sign separate leases?

✓ What if one person wants to move out early?

✓ Will someone pay more for a larger room or to use the designated parking spot?

IT'S A CHORE

✓ How will you divide up the chores?

✓ Who will do the grocery shopping and cooking?

✓ Are you a neat freak? Total slob? Somewhere in between?

✓ What level of cleanliness is okay in the kitchen? Bathroom? Livingroom? Other shared areas?

LOVIN' AND LIVIN' LIFE

✓ Do you like to be in the livingroom hanging out with friends, or would you rather be alone in your room reading?

✓ Do you like to entertain? How so?

✓ How much of the time do you like to watch TV?

✓ Do you play loud music?

✓ How do you spend your weekends?

✓ What is your work and play schedule like?

✓ What time do you get up? Go to bed?

✓ What do you like to do in your free time? Interests? Hobbies?

✓ How religious are you?

✓ How much time do you want to spend with your roomie?

✓ Do you have any loud habits or hobbies (e.g., playing the drums)?

GUESTS, NOT PESTS

✓ How do you feel about significant others spending a night—or two or three?

✓ Will you have friends or family over a lot?

✓ Will there be any children who visit?

✓ What about long-term guests?

EAT, DRINK, AND BE MERRY

✓ Do you smoke? Can you live with a smoker? Can you designate certain areas nonsmoking (the whole apartment) and smoking (the porch or balcony)? (Be sure to check your lease's smoking policy.)

✓ Do you drink? How much?

✓ Do you do any drugs?

✓ Are there certain foods you can't or don't want to have in the house?

FURRY FRIENDS

✓ Do you want a pet? If so, what kind? (Check your rental policy first.)

✓ Do you or friends who will be visiting a lot have pet allergies?

✓ Are you okay with certain pet "challenges" such as hair, stains, barking, and damage to carpeting, clothes, and furniture?

✓ Who will be responsible for the pet's food, care, exercise, cleanup, and vet's visits?

DO YOUR HOMEWORK

If you can, take your time when looking for a place to live. You may hit some special rates and get more of the amenities that you want.

Figure out your most important wants and needs and rank them, and be prepared to give up one or two of the options you'd like. How important is it to you to have a washer and dryer in the unit or on the premises? A fireplace? A carport? Community swimming pool? While it may seem more chic to live in the heart of the city, if you live even just a few miles out, you'll find that prices drop but your amenities rise. Prepare a "Must Have," "Would Like to Have," and a "Can Live Without" list using the space provided on pp. 87-88.

Some of the most important stuff to consider is finding an apartment that you'll like and be comfortable living in, that you can afford, that is in a safe area, and that is convenient to work, shopping, friends, entertainment, etc. Need a caffeine fix? Make sure there's a coffee shop within three blocks—or less—if you can't make it without your latte. Other things to consider are parking, laundry facilities, maintenance staff hours, public transportation access, workout/pool area, pet policies, and whether the units are smoking or non-smoking.

Make a list of any special considerations that you might need, such as easy wheelchair access or that huge armoire that may not fit. Take measurements of your larger furnishings (and take along a tape measure when viewing units) to see how your things will fit.

It's also a good idea to go ahead and gather all of the information that a potential landlord will need so that there's no delay if you find a place you want and they want to offer it to you. When meeting with your landlord, take along:

✓ **Your list of questions for him**

✓ **Pen and paper for note taking**

✓ **A checkbook and/or credit card to leave a deposit**

✓ **Your credit report (It's a good idea for you to look at it beforehand.)**

✓ **References, including any former landlords (Phone ahead of time to alert them.)**

✓ **A recent pay stub and/or tax return**

✓ **Your Social Security number**

✓ **Contact information for your employer**

✓ **Contact information for your current landlord (if applicable)**

✓ **Contact information for your primary bank**

THE SEARCH

CHECK OUT *FOR RENT* MAGAZINE OR OTHER APARTMENT GUIDES

These free publications are available at grocery stores and your chamber of commerce. This is a good starting point because it will show you different prices and amenities for different areas of a city so you can compare. Take this guide with you when you are looking and jot down notes in it.

SURF THE WEB

You can also search for apartments online. There's lots of apartment listing resources on the Web (such as *www.forrent.com*), and searching these sites will again give you an idea what kinds of things are available in your area and what you can expect to pay. You can choose your price range and amenities to narrow down your search results for those that more closely match what you need/want.

CALL AN APARTMENT SEARCH SERVICE

These services are free, and all you have to do is tell them the area you want to live in, how much you want to pay, and what amenities you want. You should never have to pay a fee for any legitimate apartment search service; it's paid by the leasing agents.

LOOK IN NEWSPAPERS

Check out the classified section in every newspaper that serves the area where you are looking. Sometimes small community newspapers in large cities will not have listings in the bigger city-wide papers, so don't overlook them. The classifieds are a bit overwhelming, but they do list current places available to rent. (In big cities, classifieds are often organized by geographic section.) The multiple listings for many different kinds of apartments and varying price ranges will give you an idea of what's out there.

LET YOUR FINGERS DO THE WALKING

The yellow pages in the phone book will list apartment facilities. If you're not familiar with them, you'll have to call each one for information and to schedule a visit. Also, the phone book will most likely list the bigger facilities, so you may not get a full picture of what's available.

CHECK WITH YOUR POSSE

Word of mouth is a great way to find an apartment, so let your friends, family, colleagues—everyone—know that you're looking and tell them what you're looking for. Or, perhaps you know someone who lived somewhere and loved it, and there might be a vacancy. The more people who are aware that you're looking, the better the chance that someone will see something and let you know about it. If you're moving to a new area for a job, ask your new employer's HR department for the best places to look.

People are also a good resource for references. Ask anyone you know who lives in an apartment in the area where you're looking who their landlord or property manager is. When you call the landlord, let them know a current tenant referred you.

HIT THE ROAD

If there's an area you know you want to live in, get in your car and drive around it (or, if it's an urban area, walk around it). Better yet, have a friend drive you around so you can get a good look and take notes. This is a great way to see apartments first hand, and it allows you to pinpoint areas you like and concentrate on them. Look for FOR RENT signs and property management offices. Take a pad of paper and pencil with you to write down the phone number listed and any other observations that you have.

TAKE A LOOK AROUND

If possible, it's a good idea to return to the neighborhood or complex that you're interested in during different times of the day to give you an idea of how loud, friendly, busy, etc., the place is. When driving around at night, check to see if there's adequate lighting and look for any bushes or other obstacles that might present a safety issue. Look to see if trash is removed, that the grounds are kept up, that there's adequate parking and trash receptacles, and that the general upkeep is okay.

This will also give you a chance to meet some of the neighbors if they're out and about and see if you feel as though you'd be a good fit. Ask them what they think of their place *and* their landlord. Tell them you're looking at an apartment in the complex and ask if you can ask them some questions about the landlord. If they seem reluctant, let it drop, but keep their hesitancy in mind if you decide to talk to the landlord. Don't ever ask to go inside—for your safety and theirs.

If you do talk to current tenants, ask specific questions: how promptly service requests are answered, how well the buildings are maintained, how responsive the landlord is to complaints, if the landlord responds to emergency calls after office hours in a timely manner, how much the rent increases annually on average, and if the management is responsive to other issues.

Once you've found a place that appeals to you on the outside, it's time to take a look inside. Schedule a time with the management to be shown the inside, preferably during the day—you'll want to see how much natural light the place gets. Seeing it during the day will also show you what shape the place is in and whether more work is needed to make it livable.

Pay attention to things: When you look at the unit, don't let the agent's incessant chattering about it, the current tenant's cool furnishings, or a fresh coat of paint keep you from looking at the details (neither should you let the current tenant's prized beer can collection or sloppy housekeeping distract you). Open cabinets, turn on faucets, look in the closets, check out the plumbing and hardware fixtures, and examine the walls, floors, and appliances. If there's something you'd like replaced or fixed, ask about it then. Keep your eyes open, trust your instincts, and pay attention to detail, and you'll have a pretty good idea what you're getting yourself into with a new place.

Here is a checklist of things to look for:

SAFETY DANCE

✓ Are the locks on the entrance door of the building and on the door to the apartment in good condition? Check the doors for signs of break-ins.

✓ How would you shut off the electricity and the water in case of an emergency?

✓ Is there enough lighting outside leading up to your outside door?

✓ Are there locks on any windows at street level?

✓ Are there fire exits in the back and front of the building? How would you get out of the building in case of fire? (Make sure that fire exits are not blocked or used as storage space.)

✓ Is there a smoke detector in the apartment and hallway?

GIMMEE SOME SPACE

✓ Is there enough cupboard and drawer space to hold everybody's stuff (dishes, food, small appliances)?

✓ Are the bedrooms big enough for your own personal things, such as a computer desk, a double bed, a night-stand, and a dresser?

✓ Is there enough closet space for everything (clothes, linens, coats, storage)?

✓ Is the common area big enough for everything?

AMEN TO AMENITIES

✓ Are there laundry facilities in the building or unit?

✓ Are common facilities (pools, recreation rooms, laundry) clean, well-maintained, and up-to-date?

DETAILS, DETAILS

✓ Does everything in the place seem to work correctly? (Check doorbells, flush toilets, test thermostats, run the shower, and check the windows and doors.)

✓ Do all the appliances work (ice in the freezer, an oven that heats okay, burners that heat evenly)?

✓ Are the counters, walls, floors, and ceiling clean and in good repair?

✓ Do the doors, drawers, and closets open and shut properly?

✓ Check the taps for hot water and the water pressure. Are the drains clogged?

✓ Are the sinks and bathtub cracked or leaking? Check for water damage.

✓ Is there rust in the sinks, mold on the pipes, or leaking faucets? (These are all evidence of poor plumbing.)

✓ Are there three-pronged electrical outlets in every room and enough electrical outlets for all of your lamps and appliances?

ALL THE COMFORTS OF HOME

✓ Is the kitchen all right for your cooking needs?

✓ Are there enough windows (enough lighting) in the place?

✓ What floor is your apartment located on, and what floor do you prefer to be on? (Units on upper floors can be a pain when hauling stuff inside, but some people feel safer. Units on lower floors may have noise from above, and units on the corners may have more walls exposed to the outside that could affect the temperature inside the unit.)

✓ How is the noise level of the unit? Stand in one room, and have someone else talk in a different room. This will help test how soundproof the walls are.

✓ How is the noise level outside the unit? Is it near a busy street and do you hear traffic?

✓ How is the unit heated? Do you control the thermostat? Are there ducts in every room?

✓ Is there carpeting? A dishwasher? Cable hook-up?

✓ Are there radiators or heating ducts in each room?

✓ Is it well insulated? Check to see if the windows fit properly. The number of outside "faces" (roof, outer walls) the apartment has will also affect heating costs.

✓ Is there proper ventilation? Do all the windows in the unit open?

Tiptoe and tap dance through any unit you're serious about. If you see things that aren't cool, point them out to the landlord and ask what he plans to do about it. The best time to ask about repairs and improvements is *before* you commit.

MEET YOUR LANDLORD

If you think you've found The Place, you'll want to schedule a meeting with the landlord/leasing agent. You need to make a good impression, provide the landlord with information he or she needs, and ask the questions you need answered. Being prepared will not only make a positive impression, but will make sure you get all the 411 you need to make your decision.

When you call to schedule a visit and/or interview, make sure to get the name and direct phone number of the person you will be meeting with. When you meet with a prospective landlord, take advantage of this time to get answers to your questions. Dress neatly for your interview and bring all of the documents you need. Unless you are renting with a roommate, it is best to go to your appointment alone.

Chances are you will deal with a number of people in the course of your apartment search. Pay attention in your dealings with each, from the receptionist to the leasing agent, as this is a pretty good indicator of what your future dealings with them will be like. Are they friendly and accommodating? Do they answer your questions honestly and completely?

Seeing the actual place probably answered a lot of questions, but there are still some hidden ones that you need to ask the landlord. The following lists should help you get down to business.

DOIN' THE DEED

✓ How much is the rent?

✓ How much is the deposit, and how much of it is refundable?

✓ On what conditions will you not get your security deposit at the end of the lease term?

✓ What is the policy of late rent/utilities/etc.?

✓ Can rent be paid individually among roommates? Can everyone sign separate leases?

✓ Is a cosigner required to sign the lease?

✓ When are the move-in/move-out dates? How much notice must you give the landlord before you move?

✓ What is the policy on subleasing? Lease renewal?

✓ How is rent to be paid (by mail or by giving it directly to the landlord or management office)?

MR. FIX IT

✓ Does the landlord or maintenance person live on the premises?

✓ Is there a 24-hour maintenance service? Who would you call with an emergency after hours? Is there a phone number at which the landlord or superintendent can be reached in case of an emergency?

✓ What is the policy on maintenance of both minor and major damages?

✓ Are there any known bug or rodent problems? What are the extermination policies?

✓ Does the apartment contain lead paint?

✓ Have there been any major repairs or renovations done in the past year? Are there any planned for the upcoming year?

✓ Who will be responsible for repairs, including small ones?

✓ Is a discount available if you do maintenance yourself?

✓ Who takes care of the common ground areas?

✓ Who is responsible for removing snow and ice in the winter and garbage year-round?

UTILITIES

✓ What utilities must you pay?

✓ Who pays for utilities and how much do they cost?

✓ Is heat included in the rent, or do you pay for it? (If you are responsible for the costs of heating the apartment, get more than an approximation of what these costs are likely to be—ask to see a statement.)

✓ Is the apartment heated with gas or with electricity?

✓ Are janitorial services offered?

MISCELLANEOUS

✓ What is the policy/cost for parking? How many spaces are available?

✓ What is your pet policy? Are there extra charges for having a pet?

✓ Where are the nearest grocery stores, coffeehouses, dry cleaners, health clubs, restaurants, bars, banks, gas stations, libraries, and parks?

✓ How close is public transportation?

✓ Are most of the other tenants in the building single, married, or families? Professionals or students?

✓ Is there additional storage space elsewhere?

✓ Have you or when will you change the lock on the door from the last tenant?

The U.S. Department of Housing and Urban Development (HUD) makes sure that landlords obey the law. If you think you've been discriminated against or feel that they are not on the up-and-up, contact the HUD at 202-708-1112.

Don't be afraid to negotiate. If you've found the perfect place but the rent's a little steep, see if the landlord can lower the rent $25 or $50 a month. You might have more success negotiating with a private rental instead of an apartment complex where rent has been established and people are willing to pay it.

My first apartment (the one I wrote about in the beginning of the chapter) had a blue stain in the center of the livingroom carpet. I knew I'd be covering it with a throw rug, so I asked the landlord if he'd take $15 off the rent because of the stain and he did. So basically just by asking a question, I covered my renter's insurance for the year!

UPON CLOSER INSPECTION . . .

Inspecting your new apartment before you sign a lease or move in is important because you can put in writing any existing problems so you don't get "docked" for them when you leave. It will also give you a chance to get any serious problems fixed before you settle in.

Take a camera with you and photograph any existing damage to the apartment. Videotaping your walkthrough will provide a visual accompaniment to your written notes. Have a friend go with you to inspect—she may catch that broken medicine cabinet mirror that you overlooked. If your landlord gave you an apartment inspection sheet, note all problems, no matter how small. If he didn't, write a formal letter noting the problems you found. Ask your landlord to repair any problems you want taken care of as soon as possible, and keep copies of all correspondence with your landlord.

Attach the inspection sheet to the lease and have it initialed by your landlord so you're not held responsible later. I once moved into an apartment building that had a large tear in the floor from where a large appliance had been dragged across during the installation. Even though I had noted it on the sheet when I moved in, they tried to charge me for it when I moved out. Fortunately, when I pointed this out to them, they did drop the charge.

Ideally, inspecting, documenting, and getting things repaired should all be done *before* you sign a lease. Be sure to make a copy for yourself.

Here is a checklist of things to look over before signing your lease and moving in:

✓ **Walls and ceilings—Make a note of any dents, holes, or cracks in the plaster; scuff marks that don't rub off; and tears, bubbles, or peeling wallpaper.**

✓ **Floors—Make a note of stains or discoloration in carpets; tears in linoleum; cracked or chipped tiles; and dents, scuffs, or stains on hardwood floors.**

✓ **Trim—Check moldings, door- and windowsills, and door and window frames for stains, cracks, leaks, or other problems.**

✓ **Electrical outlets and lights—Make sure they are working; pay close attention to any two- or three-way light switches and dimmers; ask that any burned-out bulbs be replaced.**

✓ **Bathroom(s)—Make sure all faucets (hot and cold) work without leaking; check for chips or scratches in fixtures and tile; check countertops for dents, scratches, or stains; make sure cabinets and drawers open and close properly.**

✓ Kitchen—Make sure all faucets (hot and cold) work without leaking and that the garbage disposal (if there is one) works; check for chips or scratches in fixtures and tile; check countertops for dents, scratches, or stains; make sure all appliances work and are clean; make sure cabinets and drawers open and close properly.

✓ Exterior doors and windows—Make sure they work, seal properly, and have working locks; be especially alert to evidence of water infiltration.

✓ Deck, balcony, or patio—Check for chipped flagstone, warped or cracked boards, or problems with exterior siding.

✓ Storage area—Make sure it is cleaned out and that the locks are secure.

✓ Smoke and carbon monoxide detectors—Make sure they work.

✓ Trash—Make sure any in and around the unit has been removed.

SIGNING ON THE DOTTED LINE

In addition to ponying up the first month's rent upfront, you'll also be asked to pay a security deposit to cover any damages that occur during your stay. A security deposit is usually half or all of a month's rent. So, if your rent is $500 a month, you could have to shell out $750 or $1,000 before you ever move in. You should get your deposit back when you move out, but landlords are notorious for charging you for something and keeping the dough you're due. Avoid this as best you can by not damaging anything in your unit (carpet damage, nail holes, stains).

You'll also probably have an additional pet deposit if you bring Fluffy with you. Pet deposits can be fairly steep and apartment dwellers tend to be restricted on the size and type of pet, so be sure to understand your landlord's pet policy. Don't even think about sneaking your pet in. If you're caught—which can easily happen if a cat is seen in the window, a dog barks, or a maintenance man is in your apartment doing repairs—you and Fluffy could be out on the street.

Always read a lease completely before signing it, and consult someone with legal or real-estate experience if there's something you don't understand. Review the checklists above, especially regarding lease details, maintenance, and utilities. Pay close attention to any fees or fines that are noted in the agreement. If something isn't specified, ask about it and then get it in writing. Be sure to know the terms of your agreement because leases can often be difficult to get out of. Get a copy of the rental policy which lists all rules that apply.

Don't be pressured by a landlord to sign a lease before you're ready. Sometimes they'll tell you someone else is ready to sign and you'll lose it if you don't sign right away. If you're faced with this red flag, pass. The landlord may be trying to rush you because the lease isn't in your best interest or because there's a good reason no one wants the apartment.

Once you've signed your lease, the first thing you'll want to do is purchase renter's insurance. *Always* buy renter's insurance, which is often as low as $15 a month. This small fee protects you against natural disasters, theft, or other unfortunate incidents that could destroy some or all of your belongings (see chapter 10 for more information).

The majority (if not all) of your utilities will need to be

hooked up in your new place. Call the gas, electric, cable, phone, and water companies and have your utilities hooked up the day *before* you move in.

You'll want to drop by the post office and fill out a change of address card so that mail can be forwarded. Also, be sure to contact your HR person at work and call anyone you do business with (your bank, your insurance agent, your credit card company) and let them know your new address—and don't forget to notify any magazines you subscribe to as well. Send out a mass e-mail of your new address to family and friends. If you're moving to another state, you'll need to stop by the DMV to get a new driver's license and plates for your car.

Unless you have some big burly friends you can persuade to move your furniture, you'll have to hire movers. Check the yellow pages for movers who specialize in apartment moving, and call your local Better Business Bureau to make sure they have a satisfactory rating. Reputable movers often give you an accurate quote over the phone if you tell them the furniture and number of boxes that you have to move. If you can, move the smaller stuff yourself and have them move the big stuff like furniture, which tends to be $10–$15 an item (if it's all being moved from one location), plus a possible additional fee depending on how far they have to move everything.

What would you like about living at home?

....

....

What would you like about having your own place?

....

....

Or having a roomie?

....

....

After a little bit of financial acrobatics, what can you afford to pay in rent, realistically? (A good rule of thumb is to spend no more than 25 percent of your monthly gross income—your income before taxes and other deductions.)

....

....

APARTMENT SEARCH!

Must Have:

....

....

....

....

Would Like to Have:

....

....

....

....

....

....

....

Can Live Without:

....

....

....

....

....

....

....

4

Furnishing and Decorating Your New Place

Have nothing in your house that you do not know to be useful, or believe to be beautiful.

—WILLIAM MORRIS,
BRITISH ARTIST AND WRITER

MY DAD AND I HAD JUST LOADED HIS TRUCK WITH MY THINGS FROM THE THETA HOUSE AFTER MY LAST SEMESTER in college and were driving down the street on campus. I spied what appeared to be a discarded lamp lying by the curb in front of the ATO fraternity house, and I jumped out, grabbed it, and threw it in the back of the truck. It didn't have a base, but when we screwed in a light bulb, it worked. My dad and I spent about $2 on hardware to make a base out of a block of wood and some brackets, and then we spray-painted the whole thing white. I enjoyed reading many a book by that thrifty floor lamp in my first apartment.

You finally have a place to call your own even if you're not sure what to call it. A pad. Crib. Humble abode. Mi casa. Even if it's smaller than your parents' house and more institutional than your dorm room, it's *yours*. The only problem is, it's kind of empty. But, you don't have a lot of money, you're kind of busy, your landlord has rules, and the only thing you know about feng shui is that it isn't on the Chinese takeout menu.

For the majority of people, the first place of their own is an apartment. This chapter is written with this in mind, but the information is applicable for a house or even renting a room in someone else's home. Just because you're on a shoestring budget doesn't mean you have to be hamstrung when it comes to having a really cool place. More than just making your place livable, you probably want to furnish and decorate it so you can entertain your friends and have a place you love to come home to. (Note: It is imperative to check with your landlord and review your lease before doing *anything* to your apartment, especially the walls. Not doing so could cost you big bucks to repair later.)

LOOK BEFORE YOU LEAP

First, evaluate the place and the space. One of the good things about most apartments today is that they're usually neutral, so you're starting with a blank canvas. Just about anything you want to create on this canvas will work.

Take a look around your new surroundings and make a list of its aesthetic strengths and weaknesses. It helps to note the pros and cons of your place so that you can play up your apartment's good points and play down its bad ones. Does it have large windows but low ceilings? Great wood floors but an awkward L-shaped floor plan? An eensy-weensy kitchen?

Think about whatever it was that first drew you to the place. Was it the cozy fireplace? A feeling of openness? A lot of light? If it was an architectural detail—such as a window or built-in shelves—make that the focal point of the room.

While showing off the good stuff is pretty easy, hiding the bad stuff can be a bit tricky. Here are some challenges you might face and a few ideas on how to overcome them:

DARK ROOMS

Brighten up dark rooms with light-colored walls, furniture, and fabrics. Use a lot of mirrors to reflect light and limit the appearance of dark shadows. Use blinds and sheer curtains instead of shades.

BOXY ROOMS

If a room is too boxy, create a focal point. Hang a large object, such as a mural, on the wall. Add a large, unique piece of furniture that's certain to be a conversation-starter. Suspend a disco ball or another item from the ceiling. Paint just one wall a different color than the rest.

LOW CEILINGS

If the ceilings are so low that you feel like the sky is falling, raise them. Use lamps that tilt upward to cast as much light on the ceiling as possible. Paint the ceiling a shimmery, pale color, and paint the walls a shade or two darker. Draw attention to the bottom half of the room with an eye-catching throw rug, floor cushions, and short chairs.

HAVE A PLAN— A FLOOR PLAN

If you're renting an apartment, your landlord most likely has a copy of your floor plan. Ask for one and make several copies of it. If it doesn't already have the measurements, figure them out yourself and mark them. If there isn't an existing copy of your floor plan, draw your place to scale. Note the locations of electrical outlets, phone lines, windows, doors, doorways, closets, and fireplaces. Measure and note your doors' heights and widths—a lot of older brownstones have very small door frames. While you're at it, jot down the size of your building's elevator, too, if there is one.

Take your tape measure and your floor plan whenever you go out to look for furnishings and accessories. Before you make a major purchase, such as a couch or bed, measure it and draw it to scale on your floor plan. If it overwhelms the drawing, imagine how the real thing will look! Keep in mind that you'll want to leave room to add other items later such as end tables, chairs, standing plants, and a nightstand.

I NEED MY SPACE!

If you raise your right hand and stand on one leg and your roommate scrunches down, you can both be in the kitchen at the same time. Okay, so maybe I'm exaggerating a little, but apartments, especially studios, are notorious for their lack of space.

But before you decide to use the trunk of your car as a linen closet, think about selecting furniture that does double or triple duty for storage. Use an old trunk as a TV stand, coffee table, or end table, and store items inside. Buy a bench with drawers underneath, or put your own coordinating baskets underneath it for an eclectic look. This will help you utilize tight spaces with elegance. Stacked rattan suitcases or hatboxes are great to stash less attractive stuff (i.e., home office supplies) and look nice displayed. (You can purchase plain hatboxes at craft stores inexpensively and customize them according to your style.) Buy the cheap, bare bones end table, cover it with a table valance, and store items underneath it. Look for coffee tables, end tables, or nightstands that have drawers or shelves to give you further storage.

Think about furniture that is multifunctional. A kitchen table could also be a home office desk—or a home office desk could be a kitchen table. A daybed, sofa bed, or futon can be a place to sit *and* sleep. (For a grand look and more storage space, put your bed up on cinder blocks and hide the blocks with a dust ruffle.) Use a bedroom dresser as a buffet table or console table. An ottoman can serve as a coffee table when you place a tray on top. Have an armoire as an entertainment center, but use the drawers for kitchen items, bathroom towels, even your underwear. No one but you will know what's in your drawers unless they're really

Table It

Whether you need a place to set your drink, display your stuff, or use as a desk, here are some whimsical ways to create an instant table:

- Support plywood on top of two cylinder blocks and paint all of it the same color.

- Top a pair of wood or metal sawhorses with a door or prefabricated wood panel.

- Use a pair of two-drawer filing cabinets to support a wood panel. You'll have extra filing space, too!

- Drape a plastic crate with the same fabric used in the rest of your apartment.

- Top an old flower cart or child's vintage toy wagon with a pre-cut glass top.

- Cover a small column (or two) with a pre-cut glass top (both can be found in hobby stores).

- Perch a serving tray atop a stack of large, heavy books.

- Equip a bed tray with everything you need and cozy up on the couch or in bed.

nosey. (In which case they should be the ones embarrassed, not you.)

Here are some other ways to maximize space when it's minimal:

ELIMINATE

Exorcise your pack rat demons. When it comes right down to it, you need a place to eat, sit, and sleep. Take care of the basics first and purge anything you really don't have the space for. Eliminate clutter and organize the things you really need.

SCALE DOWN

Instead of buying a couch, purchase a love seat. Replace a bulky free-standing bookcase with a shelf that's mounted to the wall with brackets. (Be sure to check with your landlord before mounting the brackets.) If you don't have room for a kitchen table for four, buy a cafe table and two chairs, or, create a banquette-type setting with a bench against the wall, the table in front of it, and chairs on the open side. (If the bench has storage beneath the seat, all the better.) If you need more seating than your couch provides, get some large throw pillows for casual, lounge-about sitting and keep them under the couch or coffee table.

LOOK AT SPACES IN A NEW WAY

Scout out every nook and cranny. Put a desk under a dormer window or in the corner by the stairs. Store and display pretty towels in an empty flower box under a windowsill in the bathroom. Situate a bookcase under a sloping ceiling. Use walls and the back of doors to hang hats, scarves, and purses. It's okay to have untraditional arrangements if they will work better in your space.

LIMIT COLORS AND PATTERNS

Limit the number of colors in your palette and use pale, cool colors to create an illusion of space. Avoid busy patterns on items like curtains, tablecloths, and bedspreads. Consider using clear acrylic furniture—it takes up less visual space.

DEFINE YOUR SPACE

Folding screens define space and add a vintage flair. They can dress up a room and hide a storage area. They come in all kinds of styles including Japanese, bamboo, and even picture frame screens that allow you to insert several images of your choice. A folding screen can also create the illusion of a separate room if, for example, your old roomie from college is visiting and you'd like to give her a "private" bedroom.

FIND YOUR STYLE

Think of your place as an outfit: Everything should coordinate from head to toe (or room to room); it should be functional and comfortable, and it should reflect your personal style. And it shouldn't make people gasp, unless it's out of sheer delight.

Consider your wants, needs, and taste. Do you like the style of a chateau in the south of France? A funky nightclub a la art deco? A Tuscan villa? Which room will you spend most of your time in? Do you need adequate lighting for evenings curled up on the couch reading? A good bar setup for parties? Both?

Keep in mind the difference between "theme" and "style." Themes—African safari, the beach, outer space—are fine if you're five, so say goodbye to a Hello Kitty bedroom. Style shows attitude, and lots of it! There are many popular styles to consider: shabby chic, traditional, eclectic, ethnic, minimalist, kitsch, contemporary, Old World, French country, and interest-specific are just a few. Browse home decorating magazines and watch home decorating shows to help you determine your favorite style and get decorating tips. Tear pages from magazines and keep them in a folder. (Add a copy of your floor plan to this folder, too.) Take it with you when you're out looking for home accessories and furnishings. It will also give you something to show salespeople so that they can better understand your vision and assist you.

Once you determine your personal style, weave it into every room. Avoid a circus atmosphere by minimizing styles, colors, and patterns. A coordinated look will create flow and rhythm, giving your place a sense of balance and harmony. And it can make a small place look bigger.

That said, everything shouldn't have to match perfectly like Gymboree's children's clothing sets. The odd whimsical accessory gives your place personality and tells a little something about the owner—you.

COLOR ME . . .

After you've decided on a style, you should choose a color scheme that both complements the space and suits your personal preferences. Primary colors (red, blue, and yellow) are basic and can't be mixed from other elements. Secondary colors (green, orange, and violet) are created by mixing two primary colors. All of these colors are grouped into either warm or cool colors. By understanding warm and cool colors, you'll get a better idea of what shades will best suit your purposes. Warm hues (yellows, reds, and oranges) are "advancing" colors because they seem as though they are coming closer to the viewer. They can make a room feel intimate and cozy. Cool hues (blues, greens, and violets) are "receding" colors because they appear to be farther away. They can make a room feel spacious and calm.

Here are some thoughts on color:

RED

Bright and bold, red suggests vitality, aggressiveness, and energy (think fire engines and stop signs). You can't help but notice it. Deep, subtle shades of red such as burgundy and maroon are great for livingrooms. Red is a wonderful accent color that makes open rooms seem more inviting. Cons: Sometimes it can be a bit too dramatic, and it can make a small room even smaller and a dark room even darker.

YELLOW

Sunny and cheerful, yellow is associated with creativity, intellect, and power. Bright yellows bring warmth and light into dark rooms, and pale yellows make small rooms seem larger. It's also a great kitchen color. Con: It could convey a lack of energy, hence the phrase "mellow yellow."

BLUE

Blue denotes harmony, loyalty, and tranquility. It's a great bedroom color because it makes one feel comforted and serene. It can also soften rooms that are over-bright. Con: Blue can be c-c-c-cold.

ORANGE

Orange has the energy of red with the softness of yellow. Dominant and lively, it's downright fun. Peachy oranges have a delicate effect, while brownish oranges (like terra-cotta) give off warm, cozy vibes. Con: Orange can make it difficult to relax and unwind.

GREEN

Green is the color of nature, and it's soothing and refreshing to the eye. Green can make apartments seem more alive by bringing a garden-like atmosphere indoors. With a lot of varying shades, green works well in just about any room. Con: The wrong shade of green can look lackluster and dull.

VIOLET

Majestic, strong, and grand, violet is a powerful accent color. Pastel violets take on the characteristics of red or blue depending on which is more prominent in the shade; lilac takes on blue's traits, while lavender takes on red's. Con: Too much violet can be intense and overpowering.

Choose two or three of your fave colors, and use them throughout your apartment. If you use many beyond that, your place will seem choppy and be visually distracting. For example, if you like blue and white, create a bedroom that features white walls, a pale blue comforter, and blue and white curtains and pillows. Add a bright yellow pillow to introduce yellow as a third, accent color. In your kitchen, hang traditional blue and white Currier and Ives porcelain plates, and put a bouquet of yellow sunflowers in a cobalt blue glass vase. To balance out vibrant colors, add neutral earth tones and shades of black and gray.

MAKE A WISH (LIST)

Now that you've laid the framework for your place, the real fun begins—furnishing and decorating it! Make a wish list of your "ideal" apartment and items for it, along with any accompanying measurements and size limits. As you begin searching for stuff, adjust or substitute items that you can't afford, don't have room for, or aren't able to find. Go to stores that are out of your price range and scout out things you really dig. Often, you can find something very similar somewhere else for a lot less.

Make a list of things you need and want and try to stay focused on these items. It's overwhelming when you're standing in the middle of a department store the size of a football field, and you might be tempted to buy more than what you came in looking for. Exercising a little discipline now will prevent you from blowing your budget on something you don't want or need, or have the space for.

Add fabric swatches and paint chips you like to the folder with your magazine clippings and floor plan. You never know when—or where—you're going to bump into the perfect item.

ORGANIZE WHAT YOU ALREADY HAVE

Take a look at what you already have to work with. Sorry, but your crates from the dorm room won't work. They are not acceptable Grown-up Furniture. (But you can put them in a closet and use them to organize stuff or turn them into tables—see the Table It sidebar.) Aside from the crates, see if there is anything else you can use. Use your imagination. Can you paint it? Change the fixtures? Reupholster it?

Whether you're moving from your dorm room or your parents' house, it's important to go through *everything* you're considering taking with you and toss what you really don't need or won't use. Chances are, your first place won't be very spacious, and even if it is, do you really want to fill it with junk?

If you're unsure as to whether you'll want an item, put it in a box and beg your folks to keep it for a year. If after a year you haven't missed it, have someone else give the contents of the box away so that you don't even have to open it.

VISIT AUNT BETTY'S ATTIC

Don't overlook the treasure in your own backyard, or rather, Mom and Dad's house—and Grandma's and Uncle Lenn's and your second cousin once removed. You get the idea. They may have a perfectly good piece of furniture or a second set of dishes that they won't ever use but can't bear to pitch. But, they may be happy to give it to you for *free* just to take it off their hands, especially if it's "staying in the family." Oh, and did I mention it's free?

The same goes for older siblings, friends, friends of friends, etc. Find out if your school or office is looking to unload a halfway decent desk. Many people will be happy for you to take their old stuff off their hands for the mere offer of coming and picking it up. Be sure to check with them to see if it's something they're going to want back someday and if you are allowed to alter it in any way. You wouldn't want to give Aunt Thelma a heart attack the first time she visits you and sees that her kitchen table has been painted Passionate Purple.

BECOME A GARAGE SALE GROUPIE

It's 6:45 A.M. on a cold, rainy Saturday. You're sitting in your car waiting for the garage door to open so that you can get a preview of the loot and wishing you'd brought a steaming cup of Nuts About Hazelnut coffee. But wait a second! There's already fifteen people ahead of you and even more snaking behind. What the heck? Is the president going to be there?

Secondhand sources—garage and moving sales, estate sales, flea markets, thrift stores, salvage shops, auctions—can offer fantastic bargains for many items in your home. Furniture, lamps, dishware, minor appliances, books, jewelry, and artwork are just some of the things you'll find. (Skip the shoes, though. This one shouldn't need any explanation. Pew!) Once you've landed a great deal, you'll be hooked—a bona fide bargain hunter.

Garage sales are one of the most popular secondhand sources, often because they can be a bit cheaper than some other second-hand opportunities. And they happen all the time. Here are a few helpful hints to help you become a Garage Sale Groupie:

DO YOUR HOMEWORK

Obviously, warmer weather breeds garage sales, so spring, sum-mer, and early fall are the most popular times. Most garage sales are held on Saturday and Sunday, but some start as early as Thursday or Friday. Drive around. Check out the classifieds. Draw a map of places that you want to hit so that you can use your time in the most efficient manner possible.

REMEMBER THAT THE EARLY BIRD GETS THE WORM

The opening scenario in this section isn't far off the mark. As soon as that garage door opens, it's like someone threw a pork chop in front of a pack of starving Chihuahuas. So get there early. If there's a phone number listed on a garage sale sign or in the newspaper classified, call it and see if you can get a preview the night before the sale. If you see something you like, ask if you can buy it then.

BOY SCOUT'S MOTTO: BE PREPARED

Wear comfortable clothes, like jeans and sneakers. Have trans-portation arranged for larger items if necessary, and let the homeowners of the garage sale know when you'll be back to pick up your item—do be sure you've paid them *and* that you've watched them put your item aside with a SOLD label on it. Bring cash as it's unlikely that they will take credit cards or checks.

Take your folder that has a copy of your apartment floor plan, wish list of items, etc. And finally, bring a measuring tape, a calculator, and a pen and pad of paper to keep track of measurements and tally your costs.

BE FLEXIBLE

Garage sales are not for those who have exact specifications in mind about what kinds of pieces they want for their home. If you're searching for a mahogany King Louis vanity with fluted columns, slender trumpet-vase feet, a soft bow front with a bell-flower and scroll waist line and only want to pay $20, you're going to be searching for a long, long time—assuming that you find it at all. Consider an assortment of pieces that remain within the broad parameters of that style. Can a coat of paint cover that style of chair you like but is painted in Awful Avocado? Can you replace the mohair lampshade on a great lamp base with a different one? Keep your eyes and your mind open for unexpected surprises that test your creativity. This doesn't mean that you should abandon your personal style and end up with an apartment that looks like it was thrown together from a junkyard, but broadening your horizons doesn't hurt.

MAKE A DECISION

Garage sales are for the faint of wallet, not the faint of heart. As the old saying goes, if you snooze, you lose. If you find something you like and you suspect you have a steal on your hands, snap it up. It's every bargain hunter for herself.

CONTROL YOURSELF

While you do want to snag something you need if it's a great price, you don't want to buy something simply because it's on sale. Stick to your list. Otherwise, you'll end up over your budget with a livingroom that's a re-creation of the garage sale. Clutter doesn't take long to accumulate. And, sometimes there's a reason why an item is a real bargain—because it's junk. If you're not sure whether it's a treasure or a trapping, bring along a friend and get her opinion.

TEST IT

If you're buying a small appliance, ask to use an electrical outlet to plug it in and see that it works. If it's a piece of furniture, look it over carefully. Do the drawers open? Are there any major dents or dings? Can these things be repaired easily and inexpensively? Do all the hinges work? Is it sturdy? If it's dishware, inspect it for chips, cracks, rusts, or stains. Unlike traditional stores, you usually can't get a refund on your purchases. But if it seems that broken parts can be easily and inexpensively fixed or replaced, go for it.

HAGGLE

If you like something but it's a bit out of your price range, make them an offer. The worst thing they can say is no. In which case you're in no worse shape than you were. Or if you can live without it, wait until the end of the day. You run the risk of something being gone, but you also stand the chance of getting a steal on something left over that the owners are desperate to get rid of, especially if it's a large item that takes up space.

DON'T GIVE UP

Traveling to garage sales can be frustrating at times, but don't be discouraged. You probably won't find a new piece of furniture for your home on your first, second, or even third trip. But bargain hunting is exhilarating for just that reason: Just when you think you've got nothing but rocks, you strike gold.

SECOND IS BEST

Once an insult if someone thought something you got was from a thrift shop, it's now a compliment. Shopping at thrift and vintage shops is very trendy, especially since retro is a hot decorating style. Knickknacks, vases, framed pictures, even furniture—it's all there.

One of the most addicting aspects of thrift shopping is that new inventory arrives on an almost constant basis since items are donated. After going week after week, you may get to be on a first-name basis with Joe-behind-the-counter. Leave him your name, phone number, and just a few items that you're looking for and ask him to give you a call if anything comes in. He just might do it. Or, you can give him a ring.

Flea markets (or bazaars) are usually held outdoors and are another great secondary source. Summer is a popular time for flea markets. Watch for flea markets where you live, and go online for listings of markets and dates in your area.

Another source many people forget to tap are salvage shops. A salvage shop is exactly what it sounds like—salvage materials like old pillars, claw-foot bathtubs, wrought-iron fencing, or tiles removed from another residence. They can provide architectural elements. Wrought-iron fencing or posts can be used as curtain rods or headboards. Topping an old birdbath with a glass top can make an interesting table or nightstand.

If you didn't find anything via the secondhand route, there's still hope to find furniture and save money. Furniture outlet malls offer a plethora of items and cost less than retail stores. You can also buy furniture and assemble it yourself. You might be surrounded by planks of fake wood and assorted nuts and bolts for a couple of hours, but even the mechanically challenged (which would be me) can do this. Discount stores offer an array of inexpensive pieces like dressers, bookcases, kitchen tables, and entertainment centers that come in boxes and require assembly. The quality of the furniture isn't premium, but it will look just fine and last you a few years, at which time you will probably be able to afford better stuff. If you're a little nervous about doing it yourself, recruit a couple of handy friends and order a pizza. If that fake Formica just looks, well, too fake, paint it!

FURNITURE FACELIFT

Whether it's a wine-stained couch cushion or a dingy yellow, peeling wood chair, there are many ways to spruce up secondhand furniture. Paint is one of the cheapest and easiest means of transforming a piece from ick to slick. You can make mismatched pieces of furniture look more like a set by staining or painting them the same shade. If you're a little more adventure-some, try your hand at stenciling, stamping, or sponge painting (materials are available at craft stores). Use these techniques in unexpected areas, such as on the windowpanes of a curio cabinet or on the straps of a leather trunk. You can also give a piece a new look just by replacing the handles, fixtures, panes, etc. Or, try using Rustoleum paint to update metal frames and fixtures with a spackled look. If you're really ambitious and the wood is good, strip, sand, and stain it. For fun, add pizzazz to a plain wall mirror by hot gluing a feather boa (available cheap at craft stores) around the edges.

Another way to spruce up furniture is to use slipcovers. No, I'm not talking about those uncomfortable, unattractive things that bring to mind the scent of mothballs and watching the Weather Channel with great Aunt Edith. Slipcovers now are much more chic. You can buy them, but you can also make them much cheaper out of just about any material: tablecloths, canvas, bedsheets, clothing, old curtains, quilts, blankets, and bedspreads. It's best to use something that's durable and washable. If you have any fabric damage, just work around it.

Fortunately for the sewing-challenged (me), all it takes to create a slipcover is some scissors, fabric glue for any trim, straight and safety pins, and a little patience. Straight pins will secure your fabric as you work with it and prevent gaping seams or crooked edges. Simply drape your slipcover piece over the couch or chair, do a few tucks, and secure areas with hidden safety pins. You might not get it just right on the first try, but it's easy enough to start over and try again.

To create your own slipcover design, you can use cotton duck canvas in a painter's canvas, which you can find at the local hardware store. There's also the ordinary bedsheet, which is an absolute staple of frugal and creative apartment decorating. Flat sheets can be found on sale almost any time of the year and in a wide assortment of colors and patterns. Or, buy a plain white bedsheet, and try stamping, stenciling with a laundry marker, and painting it to create your own look. Be sure to use paints and pens that won't wash out or come off on you.

To give your slipcovers a little flair, trim them with anything—ribbon, fringe, even old clothes. You'll probably never wear that sea foam green taffeta prom dress again (please, *please* don't wear that sea foam green taffeta prom dress again), but maybe the bottom of it can be cut off and used as trim for a pillow or end table skirt. You'll have a one-of-a-kind slipcover that's also a conversation piece.

While you're at it, save some material to create coordinating throw pillows, tablecloths, runners, placemats, small footstools, throws, a dust ruffle, a bathroom sink skirt, bench cushions, chair pads, curtains, vanity skirts, and/or shower curtains. When you get tired of the look, it's cheap enough that you can simply throw everything out and create something new.

DON'T SURRENDER JUST BECAUSE YOU SEE WHITE (WALLS)

If you can't paint your walls, paint your furniture. Then, choose coordinating colored fabrics for your pillows, tablecloths, area rugs, etc. Finally, add colored accessories for the final touches.

You can add a splash of color to your walls by using a white wall-sized sheet as a canvas to paint an original piece of art. Use something that you like as inspiration, such as a hobby, interest, or time of year. If you're a golfer, paint a golf club or ball, or if you love Cosmopolitans, paint one in a martini glass. Or imitate your favorite artist's style by doing a broad brushstroke of his work. The effect is a contemporary, dramatic backdrop. Even if you're artistically challenged, you can use patterns or stencils.

If you really want to create a masterpiece that will impress your friends, use an overhead projector if you can borrow one from an office or school. (Surely you know *someone* who is a teacher and can spare it for a week.) Place a plain transparency over the image you want to duplicate and trace it. Affix your

Fabulous with Fabric

Even if you can't paint or wallpaper your walls, you can liven them up by covering them with fabric. This will give you the same effect as wallpaper without violating your lease, plus it's reusable. It's a good idea to use light-weight fabrics in solid colors or patterns so that they can be easily matched.

Here's how to do it.

1. Measure your walls and choose enough fabric to cover them, allowing extra material all the way around. (Buy additional fabric if you want to make some throw pillows to match.)

2. Gently wash walls with a sponge and a mild detergent to remove dirt. Rinse well with a clean sponge.

3. Pour some liquid starch in a bowl, and use a sponge roller to apply enough starch to the wall for the first section of fabric. (It's a good idea to start in an "invisible" corner first where a mismatch won't be easily seen.)

4. Hold the first panel of fabric taut and adhere it to the wall, allowing a few inches of overlap at the floor, ceiling, and around windows and door frames. Use a large, dry sponge to smooth out any bubbles.

5. Continue to apply fabric, matching up patterns and designs when necessary.

6. Once the fabric is completely dry, trim the excess at the floor and ceiling and around windows and doors with a sharp utility knife.

7. When you're ready to remove the fabric, simply dampen it and peel it off the wall. Wash the starch off the walls with mild soap.

sheet from the ceiling against the wall, turn on the overhead projector, and project your newly created transparency onto the wall. Adjust it until it's straight on the sheet and the size that you want. Trace the projected image on the sheet, and then take it down and paint it.

Another option is to add faux wallpaper borders around the top of your walls with greeting cards, postcards, calendar images, magazine covers, sheet music, etc. Put some removable adhesive tape on the back of each, and just line them up one after another where the wall and ceiling meet—very easy.

Using architectural elements against your walls can also make them interesting. If there's room, set up an easel (you can buy one cheap at arts and crafts or hobby stores) in a corner or behind an angled sofa to display framed artwork. Place a faux fireplace and mantel against a wall. Lean a large, framed mirror against the wall, and while you're at it, lean smaller pictures against mantels, armoires, tables, and bookcases.

If you want to hang things on your walls, you can still avoid putting any nail holes in the walls by using removable adhesive tape hangers. These hooks are great for hanging other items throughout your place as well.

 HANGIN' AROUND

When it comes to hanging things on a wall, one of the best design techniques is to uniformly hang a series of three related objects or pictures. They should be evenly spaced between one another either vertically or horizontally. Or you can offset a pair of objects. Both options will create interest and a sense of balance.

One fun idea is to go online to your local public library and pull up old black and white images of your city and favorite junctures. Print them out on a color copier and frame. For a personalized vintage look, take your favorite color pictures to Wal-Mart and use the do-it-yourself picture printing machines. You can create black-and-white or sepia-toned pictures for just pennies apiece and the quality is good.

Playbills, sheet music, postcards, calendar pictures, magazine and comic book covers, or newspaper headlines will give you interesting images to frame at a very low cost. Skip the flimsy poster art frames and try the nicer, sturdier, do-it-yourself frames; you can get a piece of glass cut at the hobby store for about $10–$15. Most arts and crafts stores often run "50% off" specials on their framing, so keep an eye out for those.

Think outside the box too, or in this case, the picture frame. You'd expect to see a framed print of an airplane on a wall, but would you expect to see an actual wooden propeller? Hanging an object on the wall and surrounding it with a frame minus the glass will give it a funky 3D effect. With just a little creativity, you can think of interesting objects to hang on your walls:

* **Small shelves or sconces with teapots or small, simple goldfish bowls and live goldfish**
* **A fishing net filled with seashells, sea glass, a faux mermaid, toy boats, and other beach items**
* **A kite**

* An array of Japanese fans
* Medallions or plaques
* Small musical instruments
* Board games with pieces glued onto them
* Mardi Gras or African masks
* Shadow boxes filled with objects of interest

WINDOW TREATMENTS

While most apartments already have mini blinds on the windows, some landlords allow you to add curtains as well. Places like Kmart, Wal-Mart, and Target have great window treatments at low prices. Or, you can make your own out of bed sheets, which you can match to your bedding or kitchen or bathroom linens. If you can't sew or don't have access to a sewing machine, cheat. Simply cut the amount of fabric you need. Fold over a few inches at the top, making sure there's enough room for the rod to fit through. Hot glue the folded-over edge, and then hot glue the bottom of the edge to prevent any fraying.

To add a cool valance, select a couple of complementary dinner napkins. Drape as many napkins as needed over the top of the rod in a repeating "V" pattern to form the valiance. Pin or hot glue the napkins at the top and back of the fabric to secure.

There are other nontraditional window treatments that add flair. What about garland? No, not the shiny stuff you drape around your Christmas tree, but the stuff that's done with fruits, flowers, or ivy. Affix some atop your blinds. Or, drape some mosquito netting or gauze (very inexpensive) around your windows and tie it back with tassel ties for a flowing, breezy effect.

FIX IT WITH FIXTURES

Replacing hardware, lighting, or plumbing fixtures is a little thing that makes a big difference. You can replace generic drawer and door pulls in the kitchen and bathrooms with something a little more personal. Doorknobs can also be replaced.

Shower heads, sink knobs, basically anything that simply screws on can be replaced with something you prefer. Be careful, though: You should always turn the water off before removing plumbing fixtures so you don't end up all wet. Look for the valves under the cabinet and make sure to turn off both the hot and cold valves.

Within certain restrictions, you can replace light fixtures, such as ceiling fan globes and interior ceiling fixtures. (Make sure you turn off the power at the circuit breaker box, and consult an electrician if you don't know how to wire a light.) Decorative lightbulbs can also add a personal touch.

Be sure to measure carefully and get replacements you can install without drilling new holes. Hang on to your original fixtures as you'll want to switch them back when you move and take your purchased fixtures to your next apartment or house.

LET THERE BE LIGHT

The right lighting can add a lot to a room. Whether you need good lighting to read by or romantic lighting to, um, romance by, lighting sets the mood for a room. Be generous (but careful) with the candles when entertaining—forgotten burning candles are one of the leading causes of apartment and house fires. According to the National Fire Protection Association's 2003 report, home candle fires hit a twenty-year high in 1999 with 15,040 fires, 102 civilian deaths, and $278 million in direct property damage.

Choose lamps that provide ample light for reading and be sure that they are placed at the right height for reading. A lamp placed too high can create an uncomfortable glare, and one too low can cause eyestrain. Lamps equipped with a three-way bulb are great choices.

Hit the secondhand stores and find something unique that's certain to be a conversation starter like a lamp with an unusual base or shade. Look for a variety of lamps of different styles and heights. Be sure they are sturdy enough to not get knocked over easily. Scattering different lamps and sconces throughout your place will create a warm mood. Add dimmers if possible.

You can also buy plain lamps and white lamp shades at discount stores. Paint or sponge paint the base, and paint or stencil the shade. Trim the shade with fringe, feathers, or beads. Or you can buy hollow glass lamp bases and fill them with gumballs, Barbie doll shoes, marbles, beads, faux fruits, dried flowers, or anything else you like.

DON'T SKIP THE LOO

Even though the bathroom is sometimes the forgotten stepchild, you should still carry your style over into it. Apartments are small and bathrooms are even smaller, so apartment bathrooms can be downright puny. Minimizing stuff (do you really need four different kinds of shampoo?) and organizing what you do need is a must. A bathroom storage unit that fits over the toilet or under the sink is a great space saver.

You can also put a bought or made skirt around the bathroom sink to hide ugly pipes and store items under it. Put two or three small, stackable shelves under the skirt and store occasionally-used items. If you don't have room for a towel rack, use the space between the shower liner and a shower curtain: hang your wet towel over the rod between the liner and inside part of the curtain where it can dry out of sight.

Speaking of shower curtains, they're often the largest visual in the bathroom, so give them some thought. Shower curtains are relatively inexpensive, but you can also buy a plain one even cheaper and glue fabric trim or tassels across the top.

There's no reason to buy shower accessories at high-priced department or home stores. Instead, hit the Dollar Store for items like shower curtains, toothbrush holders, soap dishes, wastepaper baskets, and bath mats. They may not literally be $1 (false advertising), but they're still dirt cheap.

ACCESSORIZE!

Adding accessories is a small way to have a big impact, and it lets houseguests know immediately upon entering your place that they found the right address. Show off your passions, whatever they are. Displaying a collection of something that interests you—books, figurines, lunchboxes, dolls, your five-year-old nephew's artwork—is a great way to personalize your place. I collect antique typewriters and have them on display on a shelf in my study. Not only are they an expression of my interests, but I like to think they help ward off writer's block!

Generally speaking, less is more when it comes to accessories, especially in a small space. Don't cover every surface with pictures and knickknacks. Instead, choose just a few for greater impact and to avoid a cluttered look. Besides, fewer knickknacks mean less dusting!

Try grouping similar objects in odd numbers for balance and impact. Achieve greater heights by stacking some of your objects on books or pretty boxes. Arrange things in layers (front to back and top to bottom) for interest and depth. Just allow enough space in between objects so they can be seen and admired.

Look for secondhand vases, bowls, dishes, cake stands, and juice glasses to display small, pretty items in. Don't be afraid to buy mismatches—this just adds character. When shopping at your grocery store, pay attention to the glass containers that are available when you purchase items such as spaghetti sauce, jelly, and candy. Fill them with something unusual or unexpected.

You can also fill your containers with sand and stick candles in them. Candles are a dramatic statement that instantly add sophistication and go with any décor. Tea candles are a great option because they can be bought cheaply in bulk and come in various scents or unscented. Line them up on a windowsill or mantel, or group them together on a plate on your end table. You can place candles just about anywhere there's adequate space for them to burn.

Plants are a wonderful way to breathe life (literally) into your place. Philodendrons are an excellent choice—they're cheap, you can keep re-clipping them to make more plants, and they're practically kill-proof. (I once gave a boyfriend a philodendron and found it six months later at the bottom of his closet underneath dirty laundry and stereo equipment. The plant was a bit droopy, but I was able to resuscitate it.) Put plants in pots and nestle them in something interesting like a funky hat or teapot. Buy terracotta pots and sponge paint them. Around the rim, hot glue seashells, pebbles, marbles, or any other small items that won't get ruined when the plant is watered.

As previously mentioned, pillows can be made inexpensively from a wide variety of fabrics. They can be small or large and, depending on size, can be thrown on couches,

Initial It

You can personalize your pad with a monogrammed pillow, and it's easy to do. Type in the letter or name on your computer (about 400-600 size type, depending on the font you choose). Print out the letter and cut it out. Trace the reverse side onto the back of the fabric and cut it out. Attach the letter right side up to a pillow with a hot glue gun or hand-stitch it. Add trim or fringe around the initial or entire pillow for extra style.

chairs, beds, or the floor. Along with a fluffy pillow, drape a comfy chenille throw diagonally on a couch or chair for added coziness. Coordinate them with a throw rug in the center of your room, which will add warmth and pull the room together. (Do be sure to check that the edges of the rug aren't beginning to curl and that it will stay in place. Hobbling around on crutches because you tripped over your rug and sprained your ankle isn't the most fun way to spend the first night in your new home.)

CHEAT SHEET! Pros and cons of the pad—keep these in mind when shopping and decorating.

....

....

....

TO DO! Stuff you'll (really) need . . .

Bed..

....

....

Whose style do you admire? What does your own style look like?

....

....

CHEAT SHEET! Design and color ideas for each room.

Bedroom..

Kitchen...

Diningroom..

Livingroom..

Bathroom..

What existing furniture can you give a facelift?

....

....

....

....

....

....

CHEAT SHEET! Favorite bargain spots to home shop . . .

....

....

....

....

....

....

....

....

....

In the Kitchen

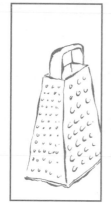

In department stores, so much
kitchen equipment is bought
indiscriminately by people
who just come in for men's
underwear.

—JULIA CHILD

MY FIRST KITCHEN APPLIANCE WAS A HARVEST GOLD (AHHHH, THE '70S) EASY BAKE OVEN THAT I GOT for Christmas when I was six. It had a timer on it, cake pans the size of saucers, and an "arm" that allowed you to push the cake into the oven where it was cooked by a big lightbulb.

Ill-advisedly, I also used my Easy Bake Oven as Barbie's tanning lamp (*Warning: do not try this at home!*). Thank goodness my parents smelled smoke before Barbie went up in flames or I might have burned down the entire Heritage Heights subdivision. Barbie escaped with minor melting, but the smell of burnt plastic lingered in our house for days. And I learned that kitchen appliances should not be used to perform salon services.

GET EQUIPPED

Your place will probably have a refrigerator/freezer, a stovetop, and an oven. If you're lucky, it will have a dishwasher; if you're really, really lucky, it will have a microwave. Hopefully you looked over the appliances before you moved in, but you might want to examine them a little more closely before you subject food to them.

REFRIGERATOR

The fridge should be cold inside, about 40°F—cold enough to keep milk fresh for five to seven days, but it shouldn't freeze. Don't treat it the way I do my purse—cramming as much stuff as possible in there. The cold air should be able to circulate around the food. (This is why your mother would yell, "Don't stand there with the refrigerator door open—you're letting all the cold air out!") Keeping an open box of baking soda in the fridge absorbs the smells. Clear out old food in the fridge every two weeks, and clean it out now and then with a sponge soaked in a mixture of warm water and dishwashing liquid. Remove the drawers, shelves, and bins, and scrub them in the sink in hot, soapy water.

FREEZER

If your freezer isn't frost-free, you'll want to defrost it several times a year so that Eskimos don't mistake it for an igloo, or worse, the buildup will prevent cool air from circulating to the fridge to keep things cold. The best time to defrost the freezer is when you don't have any food in it or the refrigerator. If it is full of food, pack any perishable food in coolers with ice and turn off (unplug) your refrigerator. Leave the refrigerator and freezer doors open and be sure to put pans at the bottom of and underneath the freezer to collect the water.

STOVETOP

It's easy to wipe down the top of the stove with a kitchen cleaner, but the part under the burners tends to get forgotten. If you cook at all, spillovers are bound to happen. When you look, you'll probably be surprised to see how much leftover spaghetti sauce is caked on. Lift up the burners and remove the liner pans. Wet with warm water, sprinkle dishwasher detergent, and let them set for a few hours. Then, use a stiff scrub brush to scrub off any yucky stuff.

OVEN

If your oven door has glass, you must keep the oven door open a little when broiling or the glass will crack. But it's a good idea to keep it cracked open regardless because broiling happens very quickly and you need to keep an eye on things so that they don't burn. Your oven should have a manual, so check that out for how to clean it. (If you don't have a manual, contact the manufacturer.)

DISHWASHER

You'll need to use a dishwasher *detergent*, not a hand dishwashing liquid, when running the dishwasher. The dishwasher is great for everyday dishes, glasses, and utensils, but don't use it for pots and pans, steak knives, or delicate items, such as wine glasses, which have thin glass stems that can break. You'll get better results if you scrub any caked-on items with a brush before loading them, and put bowls in upside down so they don't collect dirty dishwasher.

GARBAGE DISPOSAL

Even though the garbage disposal is a bit gruff, you have to be gentle with it. Only feed it small bits at a time, and don't put hard or stringy things (e.g., bones, celery stalks, banana peels) down it. Turn the water on, put just a few pieces down at a time, turn the disposal on, and leave the water running for another minute after you hear that it's done munching. Putting half of a lemon down the disposal from time to time will help keep it clean.

MICROWAVE

Nuke a cup or bowl of water for tea or soup to figure out how long things take to cook in your microwave. The biggest concern with a microwave is burns, especially from steam when lifting off plastic wrap from a container. Even if the food seems cool, it may still have hot spots. Stopping the microwave periodically throughout cooking and manually rotating the food or stirring it will help (be sure to use potholders). Never put anything metal, like utensils, aluminum foil, and fast food wrappers into the microwave. I was once so bleary-eyed studying for exams in college that I put an Arby's Roast Beef Sandwich—in its wrapper—in the microwave to reheat it. It sparked, but I caught it before I burned down the Theta house.

GRILL

I'm a Grill Girl, and I cannot emphasize its benefits enough. Most people associate barbecuing with the summer, but I do it year-round. I love it so much I'll stand outside with icicles forming in my nostrils. Asparagus, squash, chicken, steak, pork, sea bass, you name the meat or vegetable, and I probably toss it on the grill. Grilling is quick, easy, gives food a good flavor, and there are no pots and pans to clean up. Plus with a little experimentation, you'll soon establish time guidelines for your grill which will make future meals a cinch. Some apartments allow small grills, but be sure to check with your landlord first. If it's okay, make sure you aren't creating a fire hazard with where you put your grill. I personally favor true outside barbecue grills, but if you can't have one, consider an indoor grill.

Double Duty

WATER GLASS OR GOBLET Great for displaying breadsticks or small bunches of flowers.

METAL BOX GRATER Makes a pretty luminary. Cover votives with smaller graters and tapered candles with larger ones (stick the tapered candles into Playdough or clay).

COFFEE MUG Good for holding utensils and transporting them to the table.

METAL COLANDER/MIXING BOWL Works well as a bread basket or a fruit bowl.

EMPTY CAN OF TOMATO PASTE Makes a perfect cookie or biscuit cutter—just press down into the dough.

CAKE STAND If there's a hole at the bottom of the stand and a knob on top of the cover, flip both over and put the knob in the stand's hole and use the whole thing as a punch bowl.

WINE BOTTLE Wrap it in cling wrap and use it as a rolling pin.

SANDWICH BAG Snip a small hole in one of the corners and use it as a pastry bag to ice cookies and cakes. You can make your own icing with powdered sugar, a little bit of milk, a dash of vanilla, and food coloring.

SCISSORS Great for cutting pizza or snipping herbs.

Before you shell out money at a department store or home store for any kitchen must-haves, check with your mom and other relatives. They may have duplicates of perfectly good small appliances or a second set of dishes they'd be happy to give you. (Sorry, but you can no longer use your plastic tumblers with your favorite bar and grill logo on them, even if you do have a set of eighteen.)

Garage sales and flea markets are also a great place to find these things, but do be sure to plug in and test any electrical appliance. Look dishware over carefully for cracks and chips. Don't worry about finding a full matching set—go for an eclectic look and try to find just two or four from a couple of different sets. Also a lot of kitchenware stores like Mikasa, Oneida, and Farberware have outlet stores with reduced prices.

While it's really tempting to buy lots of stuff when you're cruising the endless aisles of beautifully displayed wares in a kitchen store, think about how often you'll really use something. A coffeepot? If you drink coffee every day, it's a great investment. An ice cream maker? Well, let's just say I have two friends who were given ice cream makers as wedding presents, and they're still in the boxes. And these two friends have each been married for more than ten years. Remember, there's a lot of basic equipment that can do double duty. A blender can sometimes perform the same functions of a food processor, and a saucepan can be substituted for a fondue pot.

Here is a suggested list of gear to consider when setting up your kitchen.

SMALL APPLIANCES

* Microwave
* Hand mixer
* Blender
* Coffeemaker
* Toaster

COOKWARE AND BAKEWARE

* Mixing bowls (Get microwave-safe glass, and you can also cook in them.)
* Pans and pots of various sizes
* Cookie sheets
* Cake pans (round and rectangular)
* Glass baking dishes (8" x 8", 11" x 7", and 8.5" x 11")
* Muffin tin

GLASSES AND DISHWARE

Have at least a setting of four, but eight is great.

* Dinner plates
* Salad plates (can be used for bread, salad, or dessert)
* Bowls (can be used for soup, cereal, pasta, ice cream)
* Mugs for coffee, soup, and tea
* 8 oz. glasses for most beverages
* 4 oz. glasses for orange juice and cocktails
* Wine glasses

* 2 platters (for the main dish and for side dishes)

* 2 salad bowls (for salad, vegetables, or other side dishes)

UTENSILS, TOOLS, AND GADGETS

* Measuring cups

* Measuring spoons

* Serving fork and spoon

* Can opener (manual is fine)

* Set of dinner forks, salad forks, teaspoons, butter knives, and soup spoons

* Steak knives

* Metal grater

* Colander or strainer

* Bottle opener

* Corkscrew/wine opener

* Plastic or glass cutting board

* A good set of knives

* Scissors

* Timer

* Tongs

* Meat thermometer

* Vegetable parer

* Assorted tools (wooden spoons, rubber spatula, whisk, ladle, slotted spoon)

* Salt and pepper shakers

CLEANING SUPPLIES, PAPER PRODUCTS, AND MISCELLANEOUS

* Paper napkins and towels

* Toothpicks

* Potholders and mitts

* Plastic garbage bags and seal-closure food storage bags

* Cling wrap, aluminum foil, and wax paper

* Sponges

* Kitchen towels, hand towels, and dishrags

* Matches

* Steel-wool pads and scrubbers

* Dishwasher detergent and hand dishwashing liquid

* Gentle and strong cleansers, such as Soft Scrub and Comet/Ajax

* Assorted plastic storage containers (Save peanut butter tubs and glass jars and use them for storage.)

After you've gotten what you need to set up your kitchen, it will help to arrange things in a way that makes sense. A coffeepot, knife rack, and toaster on the counter is fine if you use them often, but you probably don't need the canister of flour, any dry food, or a stack of napkins sitting out in the open—these things belong in the pantry. Most people's counters are their cooking workspaces, so it's helpful to keep them free of anything you don't use a lot. If your cupboard space is limited, decorative hooks can be used to hang pots and pans out of the way.

Once you find a place for everything, keep it there. The kitchen countertop is a pit stop for mail, extra batteries, photos, car keys, your sunglasses, that kind of thing. Find a place for this stuff, even if it's one catchall drawer you can sweep stuff

Throw in the Towel: Easy Apron

Just about everyone has a spare towel (or two, or ten!) lurking in a closet. Here's a cheap, easy way to turn that towel into a great kitchen apron. Since it's a towel, you can wipe your messy hands on it and then just throw it in the wash!

MATERIALS

- large terry cloth hand towel or small bath towel
- needle and thread or fabric glue
- 2 yards of heavy cord, twine, or leather
- a couple of 1-inch decorative beads

DIRECTIONS

1. Lay out the towel vertically and evenly fold the top two corners toward the center until the top of the towel measures about seven inches across.

2. Sew or glue the folds in place, leaving about an inch from the outer edges open to create a casing for the cord.

3. Starting at one side, thread the cord up through the casing, across the top, and then down the other side — be sure to allow a large enough loop at the top for your head to fit through.

4. To keep the cord ends from slipping back through the casing, string a couple of decorative beads on to the ends and secure with knots.

5. If the towel is too long, you can fold up the bottom of the towel on the front side a couple of inches to form a pocket. Sew or glue the pocket's side seams, and then sew or glue a center dividing seam to create two smaller pockets, if desired.

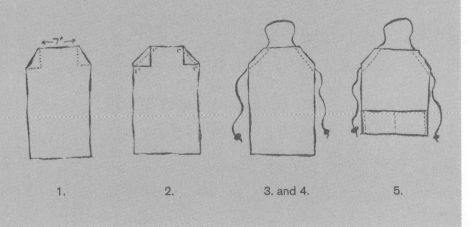

1.   2.   3. and 4.   5.

into so it's out of sight. Space is a challenge in most kitchens, and keeping yours clutter-free will help immensely.

TO MARKET WE GO

Hopefully, there's a good grocery store near you with an abundance of fresh food. Depending on where you live, there may be great specialty markets, too. Landlocked in Kansas City, I'm envious of all the fish markets on the coasts, but great steaks are easy to come by. Most cities also have farmer's markets, especially in the spring and summer, and these are wonderful for fruits, vegetables, and other homemade items. Stay away from buying food at a mini-mart or convenience store; products there cost a lot more than at a regular grocery store and items usually aren't as fresh.

Buy in bulk when it makes sense. You'll save money if you do, but only if you use it all, so shy away from perishable items. You'll probably use the larger volume of salt, but will you really use an entire case of cantaloupes? You're just wasting money if you end up throwing things away. But buying nonperishable items in bulk (if you have room to store them) will probably save you money. On the other end, buying snack-sized portions of things like candy, popcorn, and macaroni will help your waistline and keep stuff from going to waste.

Consider buying store brands instead of name brands. The labels are different, but if you look carefully, a lot of times the contents are the same. Store brands often cost less because they cut costs on things like advertising.

Try shopping once a week, and avoid shopping when you're hungry or you'll suffer from your-eyes-are-bigger-than-your-stomach syndrome. This will also help minimize impulse buying. Plan a loose weekly menu. It doesn't have to be rigid or inflexible, but seeing what you need to buy for meals will help keep you from buying items that will go bad because you'll never get around to using them. Keep a running grocery list after you've planned your meals for the week and add to it as you run out of items. Save envelopes from old mail to write your grocery lists on and store the coupons inside.

Speaking of coupons, would you take cash out of your purse, open your window, and throw it out? Of course not! But if you don't take advantage of available coupons for stuff that you buy, this is exactly what you're doing. (As I mentioned in chapter 2, do be careful about using coupons to buy something you normally wouldn't. Check out food product manufacturers' Web sites to see if you can print off coupons for items you regularly buy.)

Everyone loves to snack and everyone does it, so do it in moderation and find something else to feel guilty about. If you must indulge in junk food, limit yourself to one bag of potato chips or one box of cookies. You'll never eat it all, and your wallet, pantry, and body will all be better off.

Wherever you choose to shop, find out what day deliveries are made so the store will not only have what you want, but it will also be fresh. Here are some things to look for when you're cruising the food aisles:

MEAT, POULTRY, AND SEAFOOD

Check the expiration dates. If you get something home and it smells funny or doesn't look right, take it back with the receipt immediately, and you'll get your money back. If you're not going to use poultry, beef, or pork within two to three days, freeze it. Fresh fish should not smell fishy and should be used within twenty-four hours, and lunchmeat should be disposed of after a week. (If you defrost raw meat in the microwave, you need to go ahead and cook it since parts of it have already cooked in the microwave.)

Pass on the packaged deli meat, poultry, pork, and red meat and order from the grocer behind the counter. Not only will you get fresher food, but you can order *exactly* the portions you need—say one chicken filet instead of an entire package—so there's no waste. If you're buying seafood, ask when it came in—the answer should be "today." Also ask if it's fresh or if it was previously frozen.

Get to know your butcher. A good one should be able to tell you about the different cuts and types of meat as well as how to cook them. If you find a good butcher, ask for him by name when you return to the store. Telling the manager how helpful he is might ensure that he sticks around.

EGGS AND DAIRY

Milk products are very perishable and need to be refrigerated immediately. They should be stored in covered containers and used within five days of purchase. Reach back into the case and you'll most likely find the freshest stuff since that's where the grocer last loaded. (By the way, you can tell if eggs are still fresh by placing them in a bowl of water. If they're fresh, they'll sink; if they're stale, they'll float.) Look through the clear window in cheese packets and make sure there's no mold.

FRUITS AND VEGETABLES

Check fruits and vegetables for brown spots, soft spots, rot, and mold. Give them a sniff to make sure you get a pleasant whiff. Green vegetables like broccoli, heads of lettuce, artichokes, and asparagus should be green and show no signs of brown at the tips or leaves. Look under containers of berries and make sure there's no mold. If you're planning to use fruit during the week, buy it slightly under ripe. Mushroom caps should be smooth and not withered.

Think twice about buying fruits and vegetables out of season. Corn on the cob (if available) isn't very good from the grocery store in January, and it costs more. But pick as much as you can eat from the local farmer's market in the months when it's in season and enjoy. The same goes for apples, which are at their best in the early fall, and blueberries, which are best in the middle of summer.

CANNED GOODS

Avoid cans that are dented, have holes, rust, or are bulging. Check the expiration date. Make sure jars have no cracks and that the lids don't bulge. Select canned goods with the furthest expiration date.

WATER

If your tap water isn't safe to drink and you really need to buy bottled, buy drinking water in plastic gallon jugs at any discount store for about 50¢/gallon. It should always say, "filtered by reverse osmosis" or "distillation." It's the purest, safest, and best-tasting—and your coffeemaker will last much longer, too, since there are no deposits. Buy one nice-looking or designer brand water bottle and refill it with this if you want to tote it out. Never buy spring water—it's essentially any water pumped out of a well.

STOCKING THE STAPLES

There are some basics that you'll probably want to always have on hand in your pantry, shelves, and in the fridge. Some of these things—like mayonnaise, salad dressing, and pickles—may start out in the pantry but will need to be refrigerated once they're opened. Be sure to check the label and see. Fruit can sit out on the counter until it is ripe, and should then be refrigerated.

Dried herbs don't really go bad, but they do lose their potency after just a few months. (Some things, like sesame seeds, can get rancid.) Store herbs in a tight container (not glass) in your cupboard instead of displaying them on the counter in a rack where they're exposed to light.

Take your own tastes into consideration when selecting your staples, but here's a list to help you get started:

PANTRY

Baking powder
Baking soda
Bisquick
Bouillon cubes (fish, chicken, and beef)
Bread
Cereal
Chocolate (unsweetened squares, semisweet chips)
Coffee (beans or ground, regular and decaf)
Cooking spray
Cooking wine (white, red, sherry)
Cornstarch
Corn syrup
Crackers
Extracts (vanilla, lemon, and almond)
Flour (all purpose)
Fruit (dried)
Garlic (cloves, powder, and salt)

Grains (rice, couscous)
Herbs and spices
Jelly
Lemonade (powder)
Nuts (almonds, peanuts, pecans, walnuts, pine)
Pasta, dried (spaghetti, linguini, angel hair, fettuccine, noodles)
Peanut butter
Pepper
Popcorn
Salt, Lowry's seasoning salt
Soup (canned and dry)
Sugar (brown, granulated, and powder)
Tea
Tomatoes (canned whole and chopped)
Tuna, canned
Vegetables, canned
Wine (red)

REFRIGERATOR

Beer
Butter, margarine
Cheese (parmesan, cheddar, American)
Cream cheese
Eggs
Fruits (fresh)
Milk
Orange juice
Soda
Sour cream
Vegetables
Water (drinking)
Wine (white)
Yogurt

CONDIMENTS

Barbecue sauce
Chili paste and sauce
Honey
Horseradish
Ketchup
Maple syrup
Mayonnaise
Mustard (yellow, Dijon, spicy brown)
Oils (olive, canola, sesame, peanut, vegetable)

Olives (black and green)
Pickles
Salad dressings
Sweetener
Sauces (marinara, soy, teriyaki, Tabasco, hot pepper, Worcestershire)
Vinegars (balsamic, distilled, red wine)

It might help to divide the things in your cupboards and pantry into three categories: items you'll use every day, items you'll use a lot, and items you'll only use every now and then. Organize the everyday items in the front and the lesser-used items behind them.

I'm afraid that if I suggested you alphabetize your spices you'd laugh so hard you'd close this book and never open it again. So I'll leave that up to you. But I will suggest this: grouping things that are frequently used together—for example, baking items such as cooking spray, flour, sugar, and vanilla extract—will make things a lot easier. I've found that organizing my

Grow Your Own Herbs

There's nothing better than cooking with fresh herbs. But fresh herbs in the grocery store are expensive and they don't last long. Buy small terracotta pots (decorate them if you'd like) and grow your own herbs. While you're at it, plant a pot of pansies, too: they're pretty in their pots, edible, and look fantastic tossed on top of cakes, salads, or dishes as garnish. Some herbs to try growing in your kitchen are:

CHIVES–Great for potatoes, in omelets, salads, and soups.

BASIL–Delicious in pasta and a must to make pesto. Chop some up and add it to plain mayonnaise for a heavenly spread.

OREGANO–Fantastic in Italian dishes, especially lasagna.

PARSLEY–Great in soups and stews, as garnish, or minced and tossed on top of garlic bread and salads. Although parsley is mild-flavored, it's rich in vitamins and iron, so include it in dishes when you can.

MINT–Wonderful for tea and lamb and refreshing for drinks and desserts and is also a great garnish for both.

THYME–Gives great flavor to a variety of meats and clam chowder. It's also delicious when mixed with cream cheese.

kitchen cabinets and refrigerator shelves similarly to the way the supermarket does—one shelf for baking supplies, one spot for pastas and grains, one area for dairy—makes it a lot easier to find what I need. When I stray from this method, I wind up with four bottles of ketchup because I couldn't find the first three and purchased yet another bottle.

RECIPE READING

Even if you spent home economics class crushing on that cute guy instead of crushing up walnuts for cookies, never fear—it's never to late to learn how to cook. Enrolling in a beginners' class at the local college or community center is a fun and easy way to learn the basics of cooking, and meet new people, too. Plus, you get to eat! But if you want to venture out on your own, all you need is a well-stocked kitchen, a good cookbook, and a dash of confidence.

So you've found a great recipe that you're dying to try. Before beginning, it's important to read through the entire recipe and make sure you have a clear understanding of the ingredients it calls for and their amounts, the number of servings it makes, the utensils and equipment needed, the processes involved, the preparation time, and the cooking time. Do all of the preheating, chopping, measuring, and other prep work that you can before starting the actual cooking.

Be careful when substituting or omitting items. It's often (but not always) okay to substitute margarine for butter and cheddar

How to Make the Perfect Cup of Coffee

It's okay to occasionally indulge in a cup of joe at your favorite coffeehouse, but making it part of your daily morning ritual on the way to work can get very costly very quickly. Plus, you can probably make a better cup of coffee at home for *pennies* instead of dollars. Here's how to brew it right:

Every year or so, test your coffeepot. Fill it with water, turn it on, and let it drip into the pot. Using a candy thermometer, test the temperature of the water that your coffeepot produces—it should be approximately 200°F. If it isn't, you need a new coffeemaker.

Use good, fresh beans. Experiment with combining different beans to find your perfect concoction. Personally, I love to use three-quarters Columbian beans and one-quarter hazelnut beans for a nice rich cup of coffee with just a hint of hazelnut.

Grind the beans just before you plan to make the coffee and grind only what you need each time you brew a fresh pot. Believe me, once you've tasted fresh-ground coffee, it's worth the extra few seconds it takes to grind the beans.

Use one heaping tablespoon of ground coffee (approximately two tablespoons of beans) per 6 oz. of clean cold water. Using too little grounds will cause over extraction of the beans and cause the coffee to taste bitter. If you want your coffee a little less strong, add a little hot water to it after brewing.

Keep beans properly sealed in an air-tight container. Air and moisture are coffee killers. Never store beans in the freezer—it destroys the flavors of the oils.

For an extra special treat, keep a can of whipped cream in the fridge and add a dollop on top. For an extra-extra special treat, grate some chocolate or cinnamon on top of the whipped cream.

If you'll be toting your coffee out, invest in a cool travel mug for your hot drink.

cheese for American cheese. Leaving out a particular spice or garnish that you really detest is probably fine, but leaving out or altering the amount of another kind of ingredient could completely alter the outcome of your dish. Eggs have a specific function in cooking. Chocolate chips and almond bark look, smell, and taste similar, but they require completely different cooking procedures.

After you've successfully (or unsuccessfully) tried a recipe, jot down notes for the next time you use it. If there was a particular tool or pan that worked well, if you made any alterations that you liked, if your oven time varied from the recipe, or if you found the perfect bottle of wine or side dish to accompany it, make a note.

Sometimes you might feel as though the years of French and algebra you took in school didn't prepare you for some of the terms and measurements you'll encounter in recipes. Here's a rundown of some common terms and measurement equivalents it might help to know:

AL DENTE   Italian for "to the tooth," this usually describes pasta cooked a little on the firm side.

BASTE   To moisten with liquid while cooking to keep a dish from drying out. You can use a turkey baster or a large spoon.

BEAT   To mix by hand, with a spoon, whisk, or electric mixer.

BLANCHE   To scald in boiling water for a short period of time; blanching removes the skins of vegetables and cooks them but keeps them crunchy.

BREAD   To coat food in bread or cracker crumbs before cooking.

BROIL   To cook food close to a direct source of high heat; Always leave the oven door open when using the oven broiler.

BROWN   To cook the outside of food fairly quickly over high heat to seal in flavor and juices.

FOLD (IN)   To delicately scoop a lighter mixture into a heavier one without collapsing the final outcome.

CHOP   To cut into small pieces.

DICE	To cut into small uniform pieces like cubes.
DUST	To sprinkle food lightly with dry ingredients, such as dusting a chicken filet in a flour/spice mixture.
GARNISH	To decorate a finished dish with a smaller food item, such as parsley, capers, lemon wedges, or caviar to add color or flavor.
GRATE	To reduce a large piece of food into smaller pieces using a metal utensil with sharp holes called a grater.
JULIENNE	To cut food into thin strips or bits.
KNEAD	To mix and work dough into a pliable mass either manually or with a mixer/food processor. When done by hand, press the dough with the heels of your hands, fold in half, give a quarter turn, and repeat until smooth and elastic.
MARINATE	To immerse food (often meat, chicken, or fish) in a liquid in an airtight container and leave in the refrigerator for several hours or overnight to tenderize and seal in flavors.
MINCE	To chop into very tiny pieces (smaller than chopping).
PARE	To remove the outer covering or skin (vegetables and fruits).
PUREE	To mash to a thick, smooth consistency, often done using a blender or food processor.
REDUCE	To boil a liquid until its volume is decreased and its flavor is increased.
SCORE	To make shallow cuts into the surface of foods such as fish, meat, or chicken breasts to aid in the absorption of a marinade, to help tenderize, and/or to decorate.
SEAR	To cook meat quickly over high heat to seal in its flavor and juices.

SIMMER	To cook food in liquid gently over low heat. You should see tiny bubbles just breaking the surface of the liquid.
SNIP	To cut into small pieces with scissors, often for herbs such as parsley and chives.
STEEP	To pour boiling liquid over food (or often a teabag) and let it sit in the liquid.
TOSS	To mix ingredients gently by hand, starting with the contents at the bottom and bringing them to the top.
ZEST	Grating the very thin layer of the outer, colorful rind on a fruit (such as a lemon, orange, or lime); used to add flavor.

ABBREVIATIONS

tsp or t = teaspoon
tbsp, Tbs, or T = tablespoon
oz = ounce(s)
C, c = cup
lb. = pound
qt. = quart
pt. = pint
h, hr. = hour
min. = minutes
sm. = small
med. = medium
lg. = large

MEASUREMENTS

to taste = add a very small amount and taste;
    keep adding until you like it
a pinch = a little less than ⅛ teaspoon
3 teaspoons = 1 tablespoon
2 tablespoons = 1 ounce of liquid
1 cup liquid = 8 ounces
2 cups liquid = 1 pint = ½ quart
4 quarts liquid = 1 gallon

HELPFUL HINTS

Now that you've got the gear, gadgets, and goods, it's time to get cookin'! These tips will help make cooking easier and meals tastier. Bon appétit!

* Get fresh! The key to a delicious meal is using fresh ingredients: fresh herbs, freshly ground coffee beans, or a freshly grated block of Parmesan cheese (not the ready-made stuff that comes in a green can). The simplest meal becomes heavenly with just a few fresh ingredients.

* If you want to learn how to make something in particular, search the Internet for a recipe. Type in the words "award winning" along with the name of the item you want to learn to make and you'll narrow down the best recipe results. Visit *www.allrecipes.com*—it's a great site where most of the recipes are rated by users. I've found some excellent recipes there.

* Use a timer even if you plan to keep an eye on things. You might think that if it's 6:00 P.M. and something needs to cook for fifteen minutes, it will be easy to remember to take it out at 6:15. But it's very easy to lose track of time or get sidetracked, and a burned dish is a bummer when you've spent money and time preparing it.

* Dry ingredients are measured in standard dry measuring cups that are usually made of metal or plastic. Liquid ingredients are measured in a glass measuring cup, usually with a spout. Small amounts of liquid and dry ingredients are both measured using measuring spoons.

* Understand portions and servings. Depending on side dishes (or the size of your guests' appetites), 6–8 oz. of meat is a good rule of thumb, plus a small salad/vegetable, and a side serving of potatoes, grain, or pasta.

* Practice makes perfect when it comes to cooking. Don't wait until you're hosting a dinner party to try a new dish. Fix it a number of times beforehand so that you can tweak it to your satisfaction—and so that you'll know how to time everything perfectly.

* If you're having dinner guests, do everything else ahead of time. Set the table, turn on the music, and chill the wine before they arrive so you can relax and enjoy your time with them.

✳ Keep the kitchen clean. Not only is a dirty kitchen yucky, but it's dangerous if harmful bacteria comes into contact with food. Be especially careful with raw meat, and don't let perishable foods sit out too long at room temperature. With the exception of pulling your toenails out with pliers, I can't think of a more unpleasant experience one could have than food poisoning.

✳ Clean up as you go along. You won't feel so overwhelmed while you're cooking, and you'll enjoy your creation much more knowing there isn't a pile of dirty dishes stacked in the sink.

✳ Have a healthy respect for things that can hurt you. Knives, boiling water, stove burners, the oven, electrical appliances, and the garbage disposal deserve a lot of respect.

✳ Don't multitask. You'd hate to burn your dinner (or worse, a finger) because you're too engrossed in a phone conversation or the latest issue of *Cosmopolitan.*

✳ Open your kitchen windows and doors if you're cooking something with a strong odor (but be sure to remember to close them again for safety purposes). Place a fan in the window and turn on the exhaust by the stove if there is one. The aroma of sea scallops is wonderful when you're hungry for dinner, but it's not too appealing the next morning at breakfast.

✳ Use an extra mixing bowl as your "garbage bowl." Dump wrappers, cans, and peels in it and then empty it all at once into a large garbage pail outside.

✳ Have a smoke detector near the kitchen and test it periodically. Replace the battery when needed.

What groceries and staples are you always running out of?

....

....

....

....

....

What are your fave dishes? Do you need any special or unusual ingredients to make these?

....

....

....

....

....

What do you want to learn to make? Find easy versions to start with!

....

....

....

....

....

Which spices do you have on hand at all times?

....

....

....

....

Do you have any of your own "double duty" ideas?

....

....

....

....

From the Kitchen of

_____

_____

_____

_____

_____

_____

_____

From the Kitchen of

_____
_____
_____
_____
_____
_____
_____
_____

From the Kitchen of

_____
_____
_____
_____
_____
_____
_____
_____

6

Entertaining

Entertaining can be as simple an offering as fresh-picked strawberries and iced tea on a summer afternoon or as elaborate as a formal dinner for twenty-four. What matters is not elaborate technique or pomp or show but warmth, thought, and a sense of your own individual style.

—MARTHA STEWART,
IN HER BOOK *ENTERTAINING*

I HAD BEEN MARRIED LESS THAN ONE MONTH WHEN I DECIDED TO THROW A HUGE SURPRISE BIRTHDAY party for my husband and eighty of our closest friends. It seemed like a good idea at the time; in hindsight, I have no idea what I was thinking. I was probably just excited about my first gig as Married Hostess, and I spent weeks in search of the perfect invitations, food, drinks, décor, entertainment, and music.

The theme was Italian, an ode to Jeff's heritage. I had obsessively planned every last detail. What I hadn't planned was that *everyone* would RSVP yes and that it would be the hottest day of the year—108°F. No one would probably want to sit outside at my carefully arranged seating. And who knew it took so long to cook eight lasagnas anyway?

As I dashed around like a mad woman trying to get the main meal out on the table in time and making sure everyone was cool enough, I looked around. People were eating hors d'oeuvres, drinking cocktails, chatting, laughing, and just generally having a good time. I should have followed their lead.

I'm told that the party was a lot of fun. I guess it wasn't too disastrous because we've invited the same people over at different times since then and they've accepted. The bottom line is, if you've got a great group of people and plenty of good eats and drinks, you really can't go wrong. The key to a successful party is to be organized, plan ahead, make it easy on yourself, ask for help, expect a small catastrophe of some sort (and just go with the flow when it happens), and above all, have fun!

THE EVENT

You don't have to have a big fancy place or a plethora of matching serving dishes to host a memorable party. Heck, you don't even have to know how to cook (that's why there's takeout). All you need is the desire to have a good time.

Sometimes the reason to host a party presents itself—a birthday, Christmas, a bridal shower, the Big Game. But often the best parties are those that are done Just Because. Once you decide the who, what, where, when, and why, the rest of the party details—like the menu, décor, and music—will all fall into place. (See chapter 7 for some party theme ideas.)

Your entertaining will probably fall into one of three categories: a small, intimate affair for about four to eight people; a slightly larger gathering (say, about fifteen people); or a huge bash that includes Joe from Accounting, your third cousin once removed, and the mailman.

A small, intimate gathering is perfect for a sit-down affair like a dinner party. It's cozy. You'll probably have enough seating and full place settings, and if you don't, you can easily borrow some. For such a small gathering, either have all girls, or try to have an even mix of girls and guys. Nix inviting three couples and one single person—he or she will feel like the odd man out.

If you want to entertain a small group but don't want to spend as much money as you would on a dinner party, think about doing a brunch instead. Serve mimosas and simple but sophisticated foods like sliced fruit, bagels with lox and capers, French toast, and custom-made omelets.

For a slightly larger gathering of ten to twenty people, serving food buffet-style and having a help-yourself bar setup works well since there are too many people for a sit-down meal. To be a good hostess, offer and get your guest the first drink when they arrive and then show them where the beverages are so they can serve themselves for the rest of the party.

If you're going to have a big bash that could end up standing room only, you're probably going to want to go pretty casual. Make it as easy on yourself as possible. Get a lot of simple take-out food and serve just beer and wine (as well as nonalcoholic options). Consider enlisting a close friend as a backup hostess to help you keep an eye out that the food, drink, and toilet paper are stocked throughout the night, and help clear away any trash. You'll be busy!

GUEST LIST AND INVITATIONS

It's fun to get all of your friends together and give them an opportunity to meet each other (especially if it involves meeting single, cute new guys). But very few people are comfortable going to a party where they don't know a single soul.

If it's a small dinner party and guests aren't bringing significant others, try to invite at least one other person that a guest will know. I've become far more passive as a hostess when it comes to dinner parties because it's worked well for me: I tend to invite a small group of friends who all know each other from the same place—work, college, or an organization. There's built-in camaraderie, and it takes the pressure off of me to entertain everyone. They entertain themselves. No one has a guard up, and everyone can instantly kick back and catch up with one another.

For slightly larger affairs, I like to use the rule of three: When inviting someone, I try to also invite at least two other people that they know. So, three guys from work, three sorority sisters, the three friends from your yoga class. They'll be more comfortable immediately recognizing someone that they know and will eventually venture outside of their safety circle and meet other people once they've relaxed. It's also a good idea to try to have an equal mix of guys and girls.

There are three ways to invite people to your shindig: the telephone, a snail mailed invitation, or an e-mail/e-vite. If it's an intimate gathering, phoning guests is great. If it's a larger group, paper invitations are a good option. If it's a really large gathering and/or the event is casual, e-mail or e-vites are fine. Regardless of the number of people, I prefer a personal call or a paper invitation over electronic invitations because it's more personal. But the nice thing about e-vites is that they do all the work for you. They let you keep track of who's responded and who hasn't and who's coming and who isn't.

Still, from you guest's point of view, nothing beats an actual invitation in their hands. It's the first impression that he or she will have of your event. If you're excited about the party, they will be too. I don't mean to sound like a greeting card, but it shows you care.

You can find just about any themed invitation paper you want at office supply stores and run them through your printer. Have some fun and get creative—think outside the envelope too. If it's a tea party, make a teabag invitation by using a vellum envelope, filling it with actual loose tea, placing the invitation inside, and stapling a string and a white tab at the end of the string. For a Mexican theme, buy plastic margarita glasses and use a paint pen to write the invitation on the glass; tell guests to bring it with them to use at the party. Make coaster invitations by cutting out cardboard circles, gluing corkboard to the backs, and putting the party info on the front. Cruise the children's party favors aisle for inspiration, like hot gluing a fake watch to a New Year's Eve party invitation. You may have to hand-deliver it, but that makes it even more special. Plus you'll get to hear the first reaction of, "Oooh, how cool!"

One of the most memorable invitations I ever received was from my friend Debbie for a Hawaiian luau she was hosting. She filled a Ziploc storage bag with sand, seashells, little drink umbrellas, and other fun beach stuff, and placed the invitation in there. She delivered it in person which made it even better.

However you choose to invite your guests, include all of the information they will need in addition to the basic date-time-place facts. Communicate whether it's a full meal deal or just drinks and apps, if they can bring a guest, if there's a theme, and if there's a recommended attire. If there's a certain time you want the soiree to die down, put an end time for the festivities on the invitation. By letting people know what to expect, they can prepare for *and* get excited for your event.

EATS AND DRINKS

It was something of a novelty when price clubs first came out with ready-made hors d'oeuvres, but now it's ho-hum because it's been done. You see the same meatballs, quiches, and pinwheels at every party. Still, you can go all out without feeling put out or busting your budget.

Cheat. Don't play the martyr (besides, that position is reserved for mothers only). You don't have to cook everything—in fact, you don't have to cook anything. Whether it's a bucket of KFC or a store-bought pound cake sliced and topped with whipped cream and strawberries, no one but you has to know. Just put the food on your favorite dishes, garnish, and get rid of the evidence (that red-and-white-striped bucket with Colonel Sander's face on it). For an easy, fabulous dessert, scoop chocolate ice cream into frosted margarita glasses, sprinkle with Heath bits, pour Kahlúa over it, stick two Pirouette cookie sticks on top, and garnish with a sprig of mint. If it's a large group of people, think about getting a few different submarine sandwiches from a nearby deli, cutting them into bite-sized pieces stuck with fancy toothpicks, and resting them on top of garden lettuce on a platter. It can't get any simpler.

BYOB was fine in college, but it's time to grow up and step up.

You're hosting the party, so don't expect people to show up with their own spread. I mean, if someone is invited to a party and asked to brink their own drinks, a side dish, dessert, plus their own toilet paper (well, maybe that's taking it a bit far), then who is really hosting the party? That said, it's okay to get guests involved if the occasion warrants it. If you're having a wine-tasting party, ask everyone to bring a bottle of their favorite wine (but you can provide the nibbles).

Timing is everything when it comes to eating at parties. You don't want guests to starve by hosting a party during the dinner hour and offering only light hors d'oeuvres, nor do you want to invite people over for dinner at 7:30, skip hors d'oeuvres, and then serve dinner at 9:30. For sit-down dinners, allowing forty-five minutes to an hour from the time guests arrive for cocktails and a light appetizer followed by about a two-hour dinner works well. It gives people a chance to have a drink, get acquainted, mill about, and tide their appetites over a bit before enjoying the main

Instant Hors D'oeuvres

Whether you need a no-fuss appetizer before dinner or want to whip something up on a moment's notice when friends pop in, here are some elegant, easy edibles:

- Heated caramel-flavored topping and Granny Smith apple slices.
- Pretzel rods dipped halfway in melted white almond bark. Shake on decorative sprinkles.
- A jar of sundried tomato or olive tapenade mixed with cream cheese and spread on toasted baguette slices.
- Cucumber slices with salmon or lox, cream cheese, and capers on top.
- A bowl of macadamia nuts sprinkled with garlic salt and a drop or two of olive oil and mixed with black and green olives.
- A warmed wheel of brie topped with Adriatic fig spread and served with water crackers.
- A container of ready-made hummus drizzled with olive oil and topped with toasted pine nuts and served with pita bread.
- Boiled and sea-salted edamame (soybeans). You can buy them in the frozen foods section at grocery stores.

event—the meal. If you're cooking the dinner, don't also spend a lot of time on the appetizer (see the Instant Hors D'oeuvres sidebar for some easy, yummy ideas you can do).

If you want to just serve light hors d'oeuvres at a party but not dinner, a good time for a cocktail party is 5–7 P.M.; anything earlier and guests probably won't be hungry and anything later than that and they may expect dinner. Depending on the amount of people you have, a good rule of thumb is to serve four to six different hors d'oeuvres for a two-hour cocktail party and to plan on about six to nine pieces per person.

For a larger group, it's okay to host a party during the dinner hour and serve hors d'oeuvres as the main meal as long as they're *hearty* and there are a number of them. Plan to serve six to eight different kinds of hors d'oeuvres for a four-hour affair and for each person to have twelve to fifteen hors d'oeuvres apiece. Finger sandwiches, spring rolls, and shrimp with cocktail sauce are some easy options. Always offer a platter of cheeses, vegetables, and/or fruits—they're good fillers, easy to prepare, inexpensive, and a thoughtful option for those guests who are watching their weight or who are health conscious. Also keep in mind that it's easier to stick to those hors d'oeuvres that can be picked up and eaten with fingers (include toothpicks) so you don't have to worry about silverware.

If you offer a white wine, a red wine, and beer (plus nonalcoholic options like soda and water) at your party everyone will find something they like to drink. If you're hosting dinner, the old rule of thumb still pretty much applies: red with red

Fabulous but Frugal Wine Picks

You don't have to spend a lot of money to get a good bottle of wine. Here are some of my fave inexpensive wines to try. Prices will vary depending on where you live and where you buy, but you should be able to find most of these for under $10.

WHITE

Barefoot Chardonnay—Tempting flavors of green apples and peaches. Hints of honey and vanilla enhance the rich, buttery finish. Cool label, too.

Fetzer Sundial Chardonnay—Aromas of pineapple, lemon, vanilla, and honeydew melon are followed by crisp citrus fruit flavors.

Hess Select Chardonnay—A very fruity wine with ripe pineapple and lemon zest, backed by caramel oak aromas.

Fat Bastard Chardonnay—Elegant and powerful on the nose with hints of vanilla, hazelnut and toast. Gotta love the name, too.

Firefly Chardonnay—Rich melon, peach, and apricot aromas with oak overtones. Very cool-looking bottle.

Andretti Chardonnay—Yes, this wine is from auto racing champion Mario Andretti's winery. It has fruit aromas and flavors that hint of apples, vanilla, and spice. Perfect to sip while watching the Grand Prix!

Woodbridge Chardonnay—Vibrant tropical fruit, pear, citrus, and floral notes with spicy nuances that linger on the finish.

Trinity Oaks Chardonnay—A fresh, bright aroma of apples and citrus with a note of honeysuckle.

RED

Red Truck Red Table Wine—Red cherry, blueberry, and delicious chocolate flavors. Fun name, too!

Black Opal Cabernet Merlot—A complex berry fruit aroma tinged with a hint of oak.

Charles Shaw Merlot—Commonly known as "Two-Buck Chuck" because of its ridiculously low price ($1.99 to $3.39), this easy drinking wine is only available at Trader Joe's grocery stores, so stock up if you're ever there.

Lindeman's Merlot—A soft and luscious new-world style Merlot with well-rounded tannins and a good integration of oak.

Jacob's Creek Merlot—Soft, yet spirited, this tasty wine is fresh and easy and has fine ripe fruit flavors.

Little Penguin Shiraz—Splashes of chocolate, spice, and juicy strawberries.

Vendange Cabernet Sauvignon—Intriguing cabernet aromas of cloves, black and red cherries, and toasted oak. A hint of berry and light herbs.

Dancing Bull Zinfandel—Bright, vibrant fruit flavors and a zesty personality.

and white with white. White wines (chardonnays, pinot grigios, and sauvignon blancs) go well with white meats such as fish, pork, and chicken. People also tend to drink it more in the summer when a chilled beverage is appreciated. White wines should be served chilled but not too cold or you'll miss the flavor.

Red wines (shirazes, cabernets sauvignons, merlots, zinfandels, and pinot noirs) are fantastic with pasta, steaks, and other red meat—I love a glass with a cheeseburger. Reds are also preferred when serving most cheeses. Red wine should be stored at room temperature until opened (and served at room temperature), but then refrigerated after it is opened so it doesn't oxidize as quickly. Opened bottles of wine will last a few days (white lasting a little longer than red), but you'll need to take out an opened bottle of red wine for about forty-five minutes to an hour and let it warm to room temperature before serving.

Wine tends to be less expensive at large liquor stores, and some good vinos are even sold at wholesale clubs. Most liquor stores will give you a discount if you buy a case, so ask them if they don't offer. If you know of a wonderful vineyard with a wine you like that's out of your price range, ask the liquor store sales person if the vineyard has a second label (a less expensive line). You'll also save money if you buy the larger magnum bottles—simply pour the wine into a pretty carafe and refill as need be. Boxed wines have come a long way since they were first introduced, so consider trying some of them and tapping the wine into a carafe as well.

Offering beer and wine is perfectly hospitable, but sometimes you want to serve something just a bit more, well, fabulous. Instead of setting up an entire open bar, consider concocting one signature cocktail for your party. Whether it's mojitos, margaritas, martinis, or Moscow mules, your guests will say, "Mmmmmmm." For a cool, frosty effect, stash cocktail glasses in the freezer.

To set up a bar, you'll want to have glassware, a bucket, ice, tongs, a bottle opener, a shaker, a jigger (measurer), strainer, stirrer(s), a knife, and the appropriate garnishes for what you're serving (olives, cherries, mint, oranges, limes, or lemons). You can buy a bar tool set that should have all of these things neatly contained. For a really fun twist when serving sweet cocktails, buy the colored sugar sprinkles found in the baking aisle, put water in a bowl, wet the glass rim, and then dip it in the colored sugar. Or, use lollipops as drink stirrers. Choose colors and flavors that complement the drink (e.g., lime for margaritas and cherry for amaretto sours).

If you really want to step it up a notch or you have a very large group, consider hiring a bartender. They're more reasonable than you think. Look up state-licensed bartending schools in the yellow pages and call them for a bartender recommendation. If you hire someone, do make sure and ask them not to put out a tip jar—tell them you'll tip them at the end of the night. Or, if you have a buddy who knows how to make a mean martini, see if he'll offer his services in exchange for something else, say a few home-cooked

Ice, Ice, Baby

Whether you need ice for cocktails or to stash soda and beer in, you don't have to just use a metal tub. Use your imagination for a container that will fit your theme. Here are a few ideas:

- Child's plastic bucket and shovel
- Wheelbarrow
- Little red wagon
- Small, inflatable wading pool
- Plastic toy boat
- Garden urn or large flower pot

meals or folded loads of laundry.

So just how much liquor should you buy? Bonnie Hensley, owner of Expressive Catering, advises hostesses to figure on average for one drink per person per hour, which takes into account both the nondrinkers and heavier drinkers. She also tells people to keep the "Friday Factor" in mind. "By Friday, it's the end of the workweek and people are eager to unwind, so your cocktail consumption goes up one to two drinks per person," says Hensley. "Another subtle part of entertaining is that if people at a party know each other, they're less 'on guard' and will drink and eat more."

If you want help trying to decide how much liquor to buy at the liquor store, explain all of the party's details to the sales clerk, and he or she should be able to give you a good idea of how much you'll need. Plus, most liquor stores will let you return any unopened liquor, so save your receipt. Or, you can just keep the leftover for your next fete.

Whatever drinks you decide to serve, do make sure you have plenty of nonalcoholic beverages too, and it's not a bad idea to put on a pot of coffee toward the end of the evening either. As the hostess, it's your responsibility to keep an eye on guests and make sure they don't drink too much and that if they do, they certainly don't drive. If you think a guest has imbibed a bit too much, take their keys away and show them to their room for the night—your couch.

SETTING THE TONE

Everything from the food to the music to the décor of your party should coordinate. For example, if it's a Cinco de Mayo party, you might want to serve margaritas and Mexican food, play salsa music, have a bouquet of bright hibiscuses on the tables, hang a piñata, and paint pen guest's names on plastic maracas as place cards and/or party favors. It all goes with the flow.

FLOWER POWER

I love walking into someone's home only to be greeted by the scent of fresh flowers. They're sophisticated and often the only decoration you need for a party (plus a few candles). Floating a few flowers in a glass bowl filled with water is easy, inexpensive, and beautiful. Pairing delicate flowers like lilacs and tulips of pale shades in a cute, cup-like vase is sweet. An arrangement of red roses, delphiniums, and anemones in a tall, curvy vase is dramatic and sexy. A tight cluster of eye-popping sunflowers and Gerbera daisies is cheerful and vibrant. A bohemian bouquet of daisies and wildflowers is very hippy chic. If you're unsure what to put together, just stick with one type of flower and use plenty of it. Or, use potted flowering plants like amaryllis and violets. You'll save time since you won't have to arrange anything, and they will last longer too. (Skip carnations; they're cheap and look it.)

For a perfect, tightly clustered bouquet, I use a trick recommended by many florists. Fill a wide-mouthed vase with water. Put strips of Scotch tape (evenly spaced) horizontally and vertically across the top of the vase so that it forms a grid. Distribute flower stems equally in the squares until you can't see the Scotch tape and your arrangement looks full.

Do remember to remove the pollen stems from flowers if there are any, such as with stargazer lilies. If you don't, pollen will sprinkle everywhere and stain surfaces with a yellow color. It's very difficult to remove.

For a real fabulous but frugal arrangement, gather some small tree branches. Hot glue small varying-shaped faux fruits such as apples or lemons (found in craft stores) to the branches and arrange in a vase.

Terrific Tunes

Regardless of who your guests are or what the occasion is, here are some great CDs to toss on the stereo if you want a good groove.

- *Standard Time,* Steve Tyrell
- *Bossa Nova: Music of Love,* various artists
- *Nouveau Flamenco,* Ottmar Liebert
- *Duets* and *Duets II,* Frank Sinatra
- *Super Selections of Contemporary Jazz,* various artists
- *Mediterranean Nights,* Vehkavaara and Piltch
- *Miami South Beach Salsa,* various artists
- *The Notebook* movie soundtrack, various artists
- *Sideways* movie soundtrack, Rolfe Kent

MOOD MUSIC

Music should add a flair of festivity without dominating a party. It's best to have music that relaxes and entertains guests but still allows them to hold conversations with one another without shouting. For this reason, I think jazz music is the perfect accompaniment, and it's appealing to the majority of people regardless of their taste in music.

Classical and jazz are good for background music or to create a mellow mood, but if it's a big bash and you want to get everyone dancing, putting together a mix CD of your favorite hottest hits is a good idea. Latin music has a lot of energy and just may have your guests forming a conga line.

ENTERTAINMENT

To make your event over the top, add an element of entertainment to your party. For my husband's surprise birthday party, I wrote a song called "That's A Melcher" (to the tune of "That's Amore"). Jeff's friend Bob agreed to sing and play it on his guitar. Bob totally hammed it up and was the hit of the party.

A balloon artist, harpist, caricaturist, magician, or guitarist is a great party diversion, plus it takes the heat off of you to entertain everyone. You don't necessarily have to hire an expensive professional. What about the harpist at church, that kid who does brilliant magic tricks, that talented starving artist, or the high school music teacher who plays guitar? They'll probably appreciate a little extra money (or swapped services) and be flattered that you asked them.

LIGHTING

Nothing creates more of a mood than candles, and they're cheap. Scatter votives or use different heights of candles to create interest. Use candles of the same scent, preferably unscented candles or ones with a very faint scent so as not to overpower the flowers or your scrumptious food. And as mentioned in chapter 4, be careful where you position the candles so that they won't catch anything—or anyone—on fire.

DÉCOR

Often flowers, candles, and a well-presented spread are all you need. But a festive centerpiece or small accents in keeping with your theme are great too, such as framed childhood pictures of the guest of honor for her birthday party. But unless you're hosting a six-year-old's birthday party, skip the balloons and streamers. They're juvenile, cheap-looking, and cheesy.

IT'S THE LITTLE THINGS

Be honest. It's a little more exciting to open a gift that's exquisitely wrapped than one that's handed to you in a plastic grocery bag. The key is in the presentation. The same goes for entertaining. Whether it's the garnishes, the folded napkins, the place card holders, or the party favors, these things are like manicured hands or polished shoes—the little details that pull the whole look together.

GARNISHES

There's the standard bed of garden variety lettuce leaves you can put under foods and parsley that you can put on top. But nontraditional garnishes make a dish even more interesting. Try garnishing the top or edges of food with edible flowers such as pansies, roses, daisies, dandelions, or violets. Capers, olives, and cherry tomatoes also make for a pretty presentation, and depending on the dish, so do fruits: A fan of lemon wedges on top of fish, orange slices adorning Chinese food, and sliced limes with Mexican offerings all complement their respective dishes beautifully. And sweeter fruits like berries or mint sprigs are the perfect dessert toppings. (In colder months when fresh fruit is hard to come by, try dried fruits and nuts.)

Place Cards and Party Favors

If you're hosting a sit-down affair, avoid the Where-do-I-sit? awkwardness for your guests by having place cards. They don't have to be blah, stuffy white cards resting on holders. Here are some fun place card ideas that can also become party favors (and in some cases, after-dinner sweets) for your guests as a take-home reminder of a great time:

- Chocolate squares with names written in white icing
- Big, beautiful, flat lollipops with names written in colored icing
- Small chalkboard panels with names written in chalk (If you're really talented—and patient—try mini Etch-a-Sketches.)
- Pears or red apples with names written with a metallic marker
- Small picture frames with names written on paper and framed (You can hot glue baubles on them if you want.)
- Children's refrigerator magnets with the first letter of guests' names tucked into napkins
- Mini terracotta pots with names painted on them and raffia tied around the rims and a small packet of seeds tucked inside
- Personal-sized paper fans with ribbon through the spokes (You can write the guest's name on a paper tag, punch a hole in the corner, and tie it on to the end of the ribbon. Fans are also great for hamming it up in pictures or to use if it's hot.)
- Small "takeout" boxes with guest's names or pictures glued to the front with a bow (Fill each person's box with their favorite candies or mints.)
- Sugar cookies (slice-and-bake is fine) cut into desired shapes, iced, wrapped in cellophane, and tied with raffia or a bow with a name card attached
- Pinwheels with place cards tucked in them
- Six-packs of pansies or other pretty flowers cut into six individual trays, each wrapped in tulle with a name card tied on
- Individual collage placemats for each guest with photos, favorite sayings, and images of things they like to do written and glued on regular paper and laminated

Hensley advises making your table and the food on it picture-perfect, literally. "Pretend like someone is about to take a picture of your table. Are the best berries on top? Are the flowers fresh? Is everything arranged and presented in a pleasing manner?" asks Hensley. "Food tastes better when it looks better."

So think about interesting ways to serve and present food. Create a "veggiary" by sticking toothpicks halfway into raw veggies and then sticking the toothpick into a Styrofoam topiary from a craft store. If you're serving a side of smoked salmon, make a head for the fish out of cream cheese, put thinly sliced lemon halves behind the head to form gills, and craft an eye out of a halved olive. Put breadsticks in wineglasses and veggie dips in hollowed-out peppers.

NAPKIN FOLDING

Napkin folding is fun, easy, and will completely impress your guests. The Internet is a great resource for free napkin folding ideas. (Do a search for "free napkin folding 101," and you should get good results.) Look for Web sites that show photos with step-by-step instructions—they're easier to follow than line drawings. My personal favorite is a napkin fold commonly known as Cynthia that uses two different colored napkins. Remember, it's much easier to work with a starched linen napkin, which will hold its shape better and look nicer.

One festive favor idea is to burn CDs of your favorite music or music from the party. Put a cool title on the jacket ("Melcher's Mariachi Music") along with a color copy of a fun photo (yourself donning a huge sombrero). Display the CDs in a pretty basket by the door so guests can pick one up on their way home.

ON YOUR MARK, GET SET, PARTY!

Having a party always seems like a lot of fun—until ten minutes before it starts and you're racing around frantically like a headless chicken, chopping up veggies, cleaning the bathroom, and applying your mascara.

Do anything and everything that you can do before the day of the party. In fact, there are more things that you *can* do than can't ahead of time. Straighten up and clean your place, set up the table and bar, select the wine and music, arrange chairs, mix dips. About the only thing you can't do is prepare food that is perishable or needs to be served hot and set the ice out.

When you're preparing for your party, don't forget about the bathroom. In addition to cleaning it, make sure you have plenty of toilet paper, soap, and hand towels. If you're going to have a large number of people, put a stack of loose, folded paper towels out in a basket. Check the bathroom periodically to make sure it's still in good shape. Turn off the overhead lights, light a candle, and put a single flower in a bud vase on the counter. A small dish of mints is nice, too.

If you're having a sit-down affair, there aren't any hard-and-fast rules when it comes to deciding where to seat people, but I find the girl-boy-girl-boy pattern works well if you're having men and women. (As the host, you'll want to be seated somewhere where it's easy for you to get up and down without disrupting anything or anyone.)

Keep in mind any special considerations of your guests. My

husband and father are lefties, so I always put them at the head of the table where they won't bump elbows with other guests. Likewise, my dear friend Lynne is deaf (but a frighteningly good lip reader), so I want to make sure I seat her where she can easily see the faces of all the guests. If you've got an *affectionate* couple, put them across from one another so they can *see* one another but won't make anyone uncomfortable with their canoodling.

Remember that scene in *Pretty Woman* where Julia Roberts learns Silverware 101 from the hotel manager? Well, it's pretty accurate. People use silverware from the outside in: salad fork and dinner fork to the left of the plate, knife and spoon to the right of the plate. I like to put the salad plate and/or soup bowl on top of the dinner plate and a uniquely folded napkin either on the salad plate or in the water goblet. The butter plate can be above and off to the left of the dinner plate (with a butter knife resting on it if you have them), and water and wine goblets can be above and off to the right of the dinner plate. The dessert fork or spoon can sit horizontally just above the dinner plate.

If you're doing a buffet, consider putting large books, crates, or cinder blocks on the table, draping a tablecloth over them, and then tweaking it as you please. The varying heights add interest and drama and make your spread look professionally catered. Set out chairs where it would be inviting for people to use them, and if you need additional seating, use your outside patio chairs or borrow chairs from a friend. If a lot of utensils are needed for the food, wrap grab-able sets of silverware in napkins (secure with a piece of Scotch tape) and display them in a big basket or other container.

If you don't have a large enough table or counter space for

Party Day Countdown

One month before:

✔ Decide on event and guest list.

✔ Send invitations.

✔ Decide menu, drinks, décor, music, dishware needed, and entertainment and make lists of everything you will need and will need to buy.

✔ Secure any outside vendors.

Three weeks before:

✔ Buy all nonperishable items for party.

One week before:

✔ Call any guests who have not RSVPed to get a headcount.

✔ Purchase liquor.

✔ Decide on your outfit and make sure it's clean/undamaged.

Two days before:

✔ Make a list of and buy all food.

✔ Thoroughly clean all rooms that will be seen and used.

✔ Set up food table and bar, put out dishware, arrange chairs, do the décor, etc.

Day before:

✔ Prepare any food ahead of time that you can.

✔ Buy and arrange fresh flowers.

Day of party:

✔ Finish preparing or pick up food.

✔ Lightly clean and straighten up place.

✔ Tidy the bathroom and make sure it's well stocked.

✔ Have a place for trash.

Half an hour before party:

✔ Turn on music.

✔ Light candles.

✔ Straighten up and wipe down any counters.

✔ Set out food.

✔ Open wine.

✔ Set out ice and beverages.

✔ Put on your party dress, relax, and have fun!

your spread, buy a card table and cover it with a tablecloth. No one will ever know. It's cheap, the perfect size and height, and you can fold it up and store it under your bed or in a closet when you're through.

If you're having a ton of people and space is a real challenge, it's okay to use every room in your place—bedroom, dining-room, and kitchen. Open doors, set out trays of hors d'oeuvres, put throw pillows on the floor, and light some candles to let guests know they're welcome. If you don't want to use certain rooms but want more space in your livingroom, move the coffee table and any big chairs into your bedroom and close the door. Pile big pillows on the livingroom floor for more seating.

No matter what kind of party you're throwing, nix the paper plates and plastic cups—they scream fraternity party. If it's a huge bash and it would really work better to have disposable items, buy clear plastic plates and cups and add instant glam to them by adding adhesive gems (available in craft aisles and stores). Consider investing in a set of clear, inexpensive glass plates that will work for any occasion. I once bought a set of fifty for 75¢ a piece at an outlet store, and now I wish I'd bought more. I've used these dishes on every occasion where I've had a fair number of people—football parties, bridal showers, baby showers, birthday parties, holiday parties, you name it. So, not only do they look nicer than paper and plastic, but you'll save money in the long run by reusing them.

The same goes for glassware. Places like Linens-N-Things and Bed Bath & Beyond sell something called a "Party Pack"—nice-looking, durable, classic, clear, glass wine glasses, twelve for about $9. A case or two of these is a great investment, and you can serve any beverage in them.

A crisp, white tablecloth is always a classic; plus you can use a bleach pen to get out any stains. When it comes to napkins, paper cocktail ones are fine and festive. You can find just about any color, theme, or design that you want. Take a look at party supply stores which offer volume and selection. Or, get your own personalized, monogrammed cocktail napkins made at a paper store—it's pretty cheap to do and gives your party a personal flair.

If you want to use cloth napkins (and a matching tablecloth) for a large number of people, buy yards of fabric from the craft or discount store. Just cut out squares and use hem tape along the four sides so that they'll be smooth.

Finally, borrow a Polaroid camera for instant pictures of the festivities. Or, use a digital camera and e-mail the pics to everyone's personal e-mail account. It will make their day to receive a fun reminder of a great party.

TO DO!

What do you need to throw a party?

....

....

....

....

....

What party theme ideas do you like?

....

....

....

....

....

CHEAT SHEET! Have these mood music CDs handy.

....

....

....

....

**What hors d'oeuvres do you love? How can you easily prepare something
similar?**

....

....

....

....

....

Last minute party preps!

....

....

....

....

CHEAT SHEET!

Guest list . . .

....

....

....

....

....

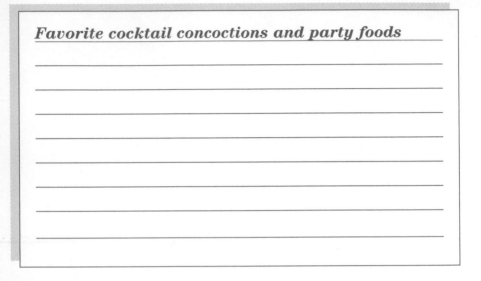

Favorite cocktail concoctions and party foods

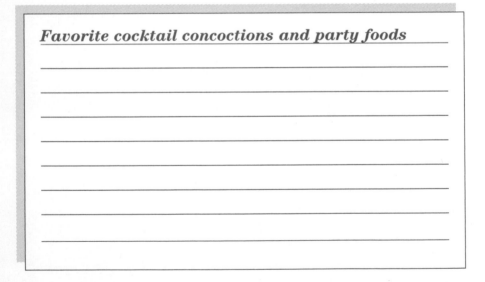

Favorite cocktail concoctions and party foods

7

Cheap Thrills

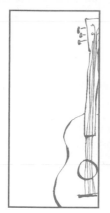

The best things in life are free.

—PROVERB

WHEN I FIRST MOVED TO KANSAS CITY, MY FRIEND CARRIE (ALSO A TRANS-PLANT FROM A SMALL TOWN) AND I MADE a pact to try something new each weekend. The Plaza Art Fair, sampling beers at a local brewpub, the American Royal Barbecue, listening to live jazz at area hot spots, and browsing antique shops in a nearby quaint town were just some of our excursions. We discovered a lot about our city and ourselves, tried new things, met fun people, and had a great time.

At this point in your life, you've probably tried a lot of new things (hopefully, most of them legal). But what haven't you tried that you want to do? That's the great thing—the possibilities are endless. So get out there and experiment!

AROUND TOWN

Regardless of how large or small your city is, there's cool stuff to do. You just need to get out there and find it!

THE LOCAL SCENE

A good first stop is the Convention & Visitor's Bureau for a free city guide of your area and brochures on things to see and do that are unique to your city (local hotels and restaurants may have these in their lobbies, too). I had lived in Kansas City for a few years before stopping by the Visitor's Bureau to get some brochures for out-of-town guests. I couldn't believe all the things there were to do that I'd never heard of!

ANNUAL EVENTS

Look at a community calendar for seasonal things like festivals, home and garden shows, arts and crafts fairs, annual events, home tours, musical performances, and tastes of the town. No matter how big or small your city is, it will have stuff. See if your company offers discounts or free tickets for these things.

COMPANY TOURS

From Harley Davidson to Dr. Pepper to Mary Kay Cosmetics, every big city has a great company that offers tours. These tours are usually free and open to the public. There are usual-ly set hours, so call ahead. You'll have a fun outing, you might get a free sampling of goodies, and you might even learn some-thing, too.

CITY MARKETPLACES

These are a fun venue for people watching, and browsing sidewalk goods and shows can fill an entire afternoon. Plus, you'll find the freshest fruits and vegetables and other homemade delights and delectables.

ROAD TRIPS

Get up on a Saturday morning and visit a nearby city after eating a big breakfast. Even if it's only twenty or thirty miles away, you don't live there, so it's out of town. Spend the day sightseeing and have lunch at a local dive. Take a camera and shoot a whole role of film of your day.

AIRPORTS

Head to the nearest airport (large or small) and pick a spot outside where you can watch the planes land and take off. Bring along a blanket to sit on, some good cheese, bread, and a bottle of wine.

THRIFT AND ANTIQUE STORES

Vintage and thrift shops offer a plethora of funky originals. Secondhand book and record stores might have one of your favorite artists or authors. Antique stores can be pricey, but sometimes you'll find a bargain. Either way, they're fun to cruise 'n' peruse. Check out flea markets and garage sales with a friend, and just for fun, see who can get the best deal for a buck.

LIBRARIES

You'd be surprised how quickly they receive the latest bestsellers. If there's a title coming out that you want to read, call ahead and get your name on a waiting list. Most also have a magazine room or area where you can read all of the most current issues of your favorite magazines for free. In addition to loaning out books, libraries also rent movies and music and offer classes.

MATINEES

You'll still get the movie-going experience but for a fraction of the price. Plus, it's kind of nice to emerge from the theater into daylight.

LOCAL COLLEGES

Local universities have a lot to offer for free or at low costs. From plays to concerts to enrichment classes to sporting events to exhibits, you'll get great entertainment value for less. Visit college Web sites to view their events calendar.

CREATIVE ARTS

Art can stir the soul, encourage self-expression, tap into your creative side, and open your mind. Who knows—maybe you'll discover you have an inner Picasso.

VISIT ART MUSEUMS

Whether it's a large museum filled with famous collections or a local artist's gallery, you'll be enlightened and inspired. Many art centers also offer interesting lectures, films, programs, performances, classes, and other events.

MAKE YOUR OWN JEWELRY

Browse the craft aisle for beads and basic cords and wires you need to create your own accessories. Then experiment until you get the end result you want. Since it's an original work of art, it will look cool no matter how it turns out! There are also many simple jewelry making books available if you need ideas to get you started.

LEARN TO PLAY A MUSICAL INSTRUMENT

Check the classifieds and pawnshops for a used instrument you've always wanted to learn to play, and check out a how-to book from the library. Trade something—dance lessons, résumé-writing services—for music lessons from a college student.

MAKE A COLLAGE OR SCRAPBOOK

It's fun to commemorate an event, party, vacay, or other memorable time in your life. Photos, postcards, letters, brochures, ticket stubs, menus, and magazine images and phrases are good, flat choices to adhere to paper or poster board. For durability, have the pages laminated at a copy center like Kinko's so they'll last. You can also have the laminated pages spiral bound together to create your own album.

GO TO A PARK AND PAINT OR DRAW

Buy a cheap easel, a canvas, and some paint and brushes at a local hobby store. Who cares if you're any good—you'll look like you know what you're doing. Maybe you'll start the next Painter's Corner.

ACQUIRE A NEW HOBBY, SKILL, OR ART

Fun classes (often called "community education") are offered by local schools and universities, boutiques, stores, and even libraries. Usually, there's a small fee for a couple of sessions. Some good low-cost classes include baking, knitting, calligraphy, singing, dancing, acting, creative writing, origami, and other arts. Come on, you know you've always wanted to learn how to salsa dance. Write that poem or short story—and better yet, try to get it published.

LISTEN TO LIVE MUSIC

You don't have to sleep outside in line, buy expensive concert tickets, stand up for three hours, shout to have a conversation, and get stepped on to hear great live music. Almost every city has restaurants (and other venues) that offer live music. While it's not good manners to go and just listen without ordering something, you don't have to order a full meal deal. Order an appetizer and drink and kick back.

LEARN A FOREIGN LANGUAGE

Whether you take a class, use tapes, or read a book, you'll become *très cultivé*.

FOOD AND DRINK

Eating is one of the few things everyone has to do and just about everyone loves to do. Good food + good friends = great fun!

HOST A WINE AND CHEESE PARTY

Ask each guest bring a bottle of their favorite wine for everyone to sample. You provide the cheeses, crackers, and fruit as well as plenty of pitchers of water. Instead of buying expensive wine charms, tie different-colored ribbons or spiral-wrap different colored pipe cleaners around the stems of wineglasses. You can even provide small notepads for people to make notes about the different vintages. If vino isn't your thing but beer is, another variation of this party is Import Night. Ask each guest to bring a six-pack of their favorite import beer, and serve pretzels, peanuts, popcorn, chips, and dip.

TAKE A COOKING CLASS

As mentioned in chapter 5, this is a fun way to learn how to cook, meet new people, and eat! Look in the Yellow Pages for cooking schools and check out community center programs and area colleges' community enrichment programs.

HAVE A POTLUCK FROM AROUND THE WORLD

Assign each guest a different dinner course to bring from a different culture—Chinese, Italian, French, German, Thai, you name it. Bonus if they dress authentically.

Say Cheese

A wine and cheese party is an easy but elegant (not to mention affordable!) alternative to a dinner party. Here are some tips for hosting one:

- Ask each guest to bring a bottle of wine. Assign each a specific type (chardonnay, sauvignon blanc, merlot, pinot noir) so that they'll go with the cheeses you're serving and there will be a nice array for everyone to sample.

- Select four cheeses in a range of flavors, colors, and textures. Good options include a soft one like Brie and a hard one like smoked Gouda.

- For the best texture and flavor, serve cheese at room temperature, not straight from the fridge. Take cheese out of the refrigerator forty-five minutes before your party.

- Leave small cheeses whole and cut larger ones into wedges. Don't cut cheese into cubes—they'll dry out and won't look as nice.

- When serving, start with the mildest cheeses first and move on to more intense ones. Put a knife out and let guests slice cheese for themselves.

- Serve cheese with sliced baguettes or unsalted crackers. Additionally, fresh fruit (such as grapes, pears, and apples), olives, and nuts are also good accompaniments.

- When pouring wine, pour less than half of a glass for each guest to sample—you want them to taste, not get toasted. Provide pitchers of water and small paper cups.

START A DINNER CLUB

Hold it at the same time and day each month. The host decides on a theme and assigns each person to bring something for it. My girlfriend JP took it one step further and turned it into a Culinary Club. Each month someone different hosts it and plans a specific topic for everyone to learn, like Cake Decorating or Cut the Cheese.

TAKE ADVANTAGE OF HAPPY HOUR DRINK AND EAT SPECIALS

Often bar and grills will offer two-for-one drinks, half-price appetizers, or other specials from 4–7 P.M. You can make a cheap dinner out of it.

CHECK OUT A NEW RESTAURANT—AT LUNCH

If there's a new restaurant that you're just dying to try, go at lunch instead of dinner. Often, it's the same or smaller portions, but the cost goes up at dinner. Plus you won't rack up the liquor bill. Even if they don't advertise it, ask if they offer half portions. Many restaurants offer such generous portions that you may have some left over for another meal. Cut your meal in half and package it up to take home *before* you begin eating, and you'll get two meals for the price of one.

GIVE YOUR FRIENDS THEIR "JUST DESSERTS"

Host a desserts-only party. Hold it after the dinner hour and have people bring their favorite dessert (bought or homemade) for all to sample. The hostess can supply the coffee, a good dessert wine, or after-dinner drinks.

EXPLORE A NEARBY WINERY
Call to see if you can bring your own picnic lunch. Pack a spread of cheese, fruit, French bread, and brownies.

TRY A NEW FRUIT
Buy some fruit you've never eaten before. Then have your friends try it and see if they can guess what it is. Take turns making up names for it.

SHARE A RECIPE
Perfect your favorite recipe (one that you're willing to share with people). Type it up and along with your name add "World Famous"—e.g., Kris's World Famous Clam Chowder.

JUST US GIRLS

Our girlfriends are often the first ones we go to when we want to celebrate a promotion or seek comfort after a bad breakup. Whether it's hitting the latest hotspot or happy hour, shopping, or just hanging out and chatting, nothing takes the place of doing stuff with these cool chicks.

SHOP—BUT DON'T BUY
Leave your wallet at home. Since you don't have any money, it's okay to look at those things you could or never would buy—a sports car, a fur coat, or fine jewelry.

HAVE A SLUMBER PARTY

My girlfriend Shannon was the pioneer of Girl's Night In. Single, married, kids, no kids, it didn't matter. We were all girls who just wanted to have some fun. Nothing says fun like blasting the stereo and dancing in your most beloved sweats or pjs, playing I Never, watching chick flicks, and drinking wine while noshing on Ritz crackers and Easy Cheese.

GET OUT THE OUIJA BOARD

Kill the lights, light some candles, put on some mystical music, and see what's in store for you. Believe, if just for one night.

ROAD-TRIP TO A FRIEND'S HOMETOWN

Discover a friend's roots by traveling with her to her hometown. You'll get to visit a new city and savor some of her mom's home cooking—and you won't find cheaper lodging anywhere.

GO TO A FASHION SHOW

Even if it's the local high school or department store, it's fun to see the latest fashions. If you can't find any fashion shows in your area, make one happen yourself!

LINGER OVER SUNDAY BRUNCH

Gather with your closest gal pals a la *Sex and the City*. It doesn't matter if you go out to a dive, a nice place, or get together at someone's house. You only have to do one thing—catch up on the latest gossip.

HIT A COUNTRY-WESTERN BAR

Completely decked out in western duds, of course. Ride the mechanical bull, line dance, tip back a few beers, and flirt with cute cowboys.

ORGANIZE A MONTHLY BOOK SWAP

This is a variation of a book club, but there's no stressing out about trying to read a required book by a certain date or preparing for intellectual discussions. Everyone simply brings a favorite book that they've read but can part with and puts it in a pile. Draw numbers (or however you want to do it) and each person gets to take home a new book. Then, turn it into a social hour.

INDULGE WITH A
PERSONAL SPA DAY AT HOME

Have everyone bring their favorite nail polishes, and do each others' nails, give facials, and experiment with hairstyles. Pass around a few copies of *In Style* and *Glamour* to inspire you.

HAVE A SATURDAY NIGHT POKER GAME

If you don't know how to play, learn. There are Web sites, books, and videos to show you how. Why should guys have all the fun?

HAVE AN OLD-FASHIONED TEA PARTY

Hold it at 4:00 P.M. (teatime) and encourage everyone to dress in their best attire. Use your (or your mother's or your grandmother's) prettiest dishes and linens, boil a kettle of water, and display an array of teas in a pretty box or bowl. Serve store-bought biscotti or shortbread cookies and fresh strawberries, or find a simple recipe for scones.

TAKE PICTURES OF YOUR FRIENDS

Add funny captions to their mugs, put them together in a sequence, and write a story, or frame your best shots as a memento of a good time.

ROMANTIC

On my very first date with my husband Jeff, we decided to go to Lawrence, Kansas, a cool college town nearby. We were having such a good time talking that we missed the exit and decided to drive on to the next large town, Topeka (an hour away), and see what there was to do there. During the drive, we pulled out the map and began choosing the towns with the funniest names and making up reasons for how they got them. I don't think it was the date that Jeff had planned, but if you're with someone great, you'll have a blast no matter what you do.

HAVE A *LADY AND THE TRAMP* DINNER

Set up a small table with a red-and-white checked tablecloth in the livingroom where you can watch this Disney classic. Cook long spaghetti and eat it together without utensils.

SHARE A ROMANTIC NOVEL TOGETHER

Take turns reading the chapters aloud. Whoever isn't reading can give foot massages.

TAKE BALLROOM DANCING OR SALSA LESSONS TOGETHER

You can either sign up for a class or get a video and have your own private sessions.

GIVE EACH OTHER MASSAGES

Consult a book or the Internet for techniques, find a scented oil you both enjoy, put on some soothing nature music, and get ready to thoroughly relax.

GO TO A DRIVE-IN MOVIE

Sadly, they're slowly dwindling, but there are still some around. Pop some popcorn beforehand to take with you. Take a blanket or lawn chairs (but place them very close together!).

STARGAZE

Sprawl out on the grass on a beautiful clear night and look up at the sky. If there's an observatory nearby, visit it for better viewing. See if you know any constellations besides the Big/Little Dipper and Orion. Make up your own names for star constellations.

WATCH THE SUNRISE OR SUNSET

Find a great vantage point for viewing and take along a blanket to snuggle under if it's cool. Bring a thermos of coffee and some fresh bagels. Ditto for the sunset and bring along your own Happy Hour nibbles and cocktails.

HAVE A CHOCOLATE FONDUE DATE

Heat a sauté pan on low and melt chocolate almond bark (found in grocery store baking aisles). Dip fruits, nuts, and pretzels. What you do with the leftover gooey chocolate is up to you.

ENJOY A CANDLELIGHT DINNER AT YOUR PLACE

Traditional, but tried and true. What better way to spend an evening than enjoying your own candlelight dinner with your honey? Set up a quiet table—even if it's the patio set outside or a picnic table—and dress it up with a fancy tablecloth, candles, flowers, and a formal dinner setting. Put some jazz CDs on and ask him to bring dessert. Wear your favorite dress and enjoy the night.

HAVE A "HIS FAVORITE THINGS" NIGHT

Yup, his favorite food, drink, movie, agenda, and hangouts. Yes, he gets to pick his favorite item in your wardrobe for you to wear. The best part? Tomorrow is "Her Favorite Things Night."

SEND HIM ON A SCAVENGER HUNT

Write clues and place them around your favorite haunts. I've made Jeff search for his Christmas gifts and Valentine's Day dinner location this way, and I get a kick out of watching a grown man scampering around gleefully.

ESCAPE TO A LOCAL BED AND BREAKFAST

Explore nearby surroundings, take a hike, savor a big breakfast, unwind in front of a roaring fire, and enjoy some quality R&R together. Try going in the off season (usually November through April and during the week) when prices are lower.

WATCH A CREATURE DOUBLE FEATURE

Turn off all the lights and watch two horror movies—and get ready to cuddle up when it gets scary. They could be classics like *Poltergeist*, *The Exorcist*, or *Halloween*, or something newer like *The Ring*. If you don't mind subtitles, check out some of the latest Japanese horror available at the video store. Creeeeepy.

SERVE HIM BREAKFAST IN BED

Include a single stemmed flower in a bud vase, fresh-squeezed orange juice, and the newspaper. Fluff his pillow. Put on his favorite music.

PLAY TWISTER

Just the two of you. In your underwear. Or less.

TAKE HIM OUT TO THE BALL GAME

April is the start of baseball season, and what guy wouldn't love being taken to a game? If major league prices are a bit, well, major league, check out minor league game prices. And most clubs also have something like Dollar Night where beer, sodas, hot dogs, popcorn, etc., are just a buck.

SELF-INDULGENT

My absolute fave way to pamper myself is to pour myself a glass of red wine and curl up with a good book or magazine. It's a great way to relax, escape reality for awhile, and soothe the soul.

BUY YOURSELF FLOWERS

You shouldn't have to spend more than a few dollars, and inhaling their sweet scent is worth every cent. Put a few on your desk at work, your kitchen table, and on your nightstand.

INDULGE IN A BUBBLE BATH

Turn the phone off, put on your most relaxing music, light a few candles, add your favorite bubble bath or bath salts to the hot water

Homemade Scented Bath Salts

- 2 cups Epsom or sea salts
- 3 squirts of body spray or 1–2 squirts of perfume
- small glass jar with airtight lid

Put salts in a thoroughly washed glass food jar (baby food jars are perfect, so ask your mom friends to save a few for you). Spray 1-2 squirts of perfume or 2-3 squirts of body spray into the jar. Cap tightly and shake gently. Ideally, let it store for a few weeks to let the scent permeate. Add to bath.

(see the Homemade Bath Salts Sidebar), and pour yourself a glass of wine. For some extra indulgence, toss a few flower petals into your bath. Have a fluffy towel and bathrobe waiting for you when you emerge.

BUY GOOD SHEETS

Wait for a white sale and buy a set of high-thread count sheets (250 or more) or try jersey sheets—sometimes known as T-shirt sheets. You'll enjoy the indulgence more every day knowing you got a good deal.

MAKE IT A MOVIE DAY

Rent or borrow several movies that you've been dying to see. Spend the whole day in your sweats or pajamas watching them. Pop some popcorn or get a carton of your favorite ice cream.

VISIT THE SALON

Get your hair washed and blown out at the salon. Having your scalp massaged during the shampooing while you inhale its clean scent is an inexpensive way to feel great and look it too.

SHOP FOR ACCESSORIES ONLY

Rather then spend a lot of moola on a whole new outfit, update your wardrobe with some inexpensive accessories like a pair of earrings or scarf. Check out discount stores and places like Claire's which will have the latest looks for less.

CREATE MEMORY BOXES

If you don't have the patience, interest, or time for scrapbooking, memory boxes are a great alternative. Simply glue a fabric you love over a cardboard box (e.g., a shoe box or shirt box). Glue on ribbon if you'd like or write on it with a fabric pen. Put special objects, photos, or mementos inside. You don't have to organize a thing.

GET A CHEAP MASSAGE

Visit the local beauty school and see what they have to offer. Whether it's a facial or foot, hand, scalp, or full body massage, you'll pay far less for one at a cosmetology school. Even if they're novices, how *bad* can a massage really be?

READ TOTAL FLUFF

Whether it's tabloids, magazines, or a steamy romance novel, it's okay—and sometimes downright rejuvenating—to lose yourself in something totally mindless.

WATCH KID TV

Curl up in front of the Saturday morning cartoons in your pjs and enjoy a cup of coffee—or better yet, hot chocolate.

WRITE A FAN LETTER

Tell your favorite celebrity why you admire them. See if you get a letter back.

SEASONAL

Although by the end of February I'm sick of cold, gray, dreary winter days, one of the things I love the best about living in the Midwest is the distinct change in seasons. Watching football games in the fall, admiring the Plaza lights at Christmas, seeing the first flowers of spring popping up, and lazily soaking up some rays on the lake in the summer—these simple pleasures are some of my favorites.

UNUSUAL OR FORGOTTEN HOLIDAYS

Everyone has Christmas parties and Fourth of July barbecues, but what about the poor forgotten holidays like Groundhog Day? Or the even more obscure ones like Blah, Blah, Blah Day (April 17), a day set aside to do whatever you need to do? If you're looking for an out-of-the-ordinary reason to do some-

Celebrate the Date

Chinese New Year
The date changes year to year, depending on if it's the year of the Dog, Monkey, Snake, etc., but it's usually in late January or early February. String a few paper lanterns and order Chinese takeout. Write individual fortunes ahead of time for guests. Find out what animal year it is, and make paper masks for your guests to wear accordingly.

Groundhog Day (February 2)
Serve "groundhogs in a blanket" (cooked hot dogs baked in ready-made crescent roll dough) and rent the movie *Groundhog Day* and watch it over and over and over.

Oscar Night
Tack up movie posters, roll out a red carpet (a bolt of red fabric from the craft store), and ask guests to arrive glammed up in gowns, jewels, boas, heels, tiaras, and the like (play paparazzi and snap their picture when they arrive). Hand out preprinted sheets listing the award categories and nominees and ask guests to fill out their picks—the guest with the most correct picks wins a prize at the end of the evening. Serve elegant hors d'oeuvres and cocktails and watch the awards on TV.

Peanuts and Pocket Lint Day (April 15)
Invite friends to stop by for peanuts and drinks after they've mailed their tax return.

Kentucky Derby (First Saturday in May)
Guests can place friendly bets on the Kentucky Derby while you serve traditional mint juleps. Have a contest to see who can come up with the most original name for a racehorse. Encourage women to adhere to tradition and don big, flowery hats.

thing fun or want a whimsical party theme, check out *Chase's Annual Events* (your local library will have it) for some real but unusual holidays.

WINTER

* **Host a Children's Classic Christmas Cartoons Marathon. Rent *A Charlie Brown Christmas, Rudolph the Red-Nosed Reindeer, How the Grinch Stole Christmas, Frosty the Snowman,* and other favorites from your youth. Bake a bunch of sugar cookies (homemade or ready-made) and cut out classic Christmas shapes. Invite friends over to decorate some to take home while you take in the 'toons.**

* **Warm up after a cold day outside with hot chocolate and marshmallows. Add a little peppermint schnapps to get you even warmer.**

* **Go on a traditional sleigh ride.**

* **Have an outdoor barbecue in the middle of a snowstorm.**

* **Check out the Christmas lights. Whether by foot or car in a city's downtown mecca or out in the 'burbs, there's nothing more peaceful than the twinkle of holiday lights.**

* **Make a snowman, a snow fort, or snow angels.**

* **Go ice skating at the nearest outdoor rink.**

* **Find the biggest hill you can and sled down it.**

* **Build a fire in the fireplace, gather some sticks, and make s'mores.**

* **Curl up and read that classic you've always wanted to— Twain, Dickens, Hemingway.**

SPRING

* **Organize a parade with your neighbors. Whether you live in an apartment complex or a subdivision, this is a fun way to get to know your neighbors. Set a time and date, distribute flyers on their doors, and put together your entry.**

* Host an Easter egg hunt for your friends. Fill plastic eggs with toy favors, plastic jewelry, candy, and other baubles.

* Visit the nearest farm. There's nothing more refreshing than clean air, blooming flowers, beautiful countryside, and baby animals.

* Sit outside at an outdoor cafe with a good book and a glass of lemonade.

* Play a really great April Fool's Day joke on someone.

* Hit the hiking, biking, and nature trails.

* Attend a garden show and learn how to plant your own flowers.

* Go to the park and fly a kite, toss a Frisbee, or feed the ducks.

* Paint your toenails a bright, fun color to get ready for open-toed sandal season.

SUMMER

* Cut a hole in the top of a watermelon, fill it with vodka, and stick crazy straws in it for friends to enjoy.

* Go see outdoor plays. Often called Picnic in the Park or Theater in the Park, you can bring a picnic basket and lawn chairs and watch a great production under the stars for just a few bucks.

* Buy a cheap, cheerful beach tote or pair of flip-flops.

* Plan an all-day float trip with friends on the nearest river. Rent canoes or inner tubes, pack a cooler, slather on some sunscreen, and have a blast.

* Host an adult ice cream social. Scoop vanilla ice cream into bowls and pour Kahlúa over them. Put out plenty of syrups, nuts, sprinkles, candies, and fruits for people to make their own creations.

* Twirl sparklers at night.

* Go to a nearby public swimming pool or water slide.

* Ride every ride at the carnival and eat cotton candy and funnel cakes.

* On holiday weekends, take a lawn chair to the best spot you can find to watch the city's fireworks.

* Hit the lake or beach. Walk along the shore, pick up seashells or interesting rocks, and make sand castles.

* Enjoy outdoor music concerts.

* If you can't afford camping equipment (or don't have any you can borrow), you can at least afford a campsite. They're free or cost just a couple of dollars. Build a huge bonfire and roast hotdogs on sticks.

* Learn how to make a mouthwatering burger and host a barbecue.

FALL

* Knit a sweater or scarf for yourself or for someone you love. (If you've never knitted, you might want to start it in the summer!)

* Host a Premiere Party for the biggest night of television series premieres.

* Go on a hayride. Bring along a thermos of hot apple cider spiced with a bit of cinnamon schnapps.

* Take a Fall Foliage tour. Even if it's just walking around a local college campus or park, enjoy the beauty of the leaves and their crunch underfoot.

* Learn the game of football so you can enjoy college and pro game days.

* Put together the most fabulous Halloween outfit you can imagine. Whether you go to a party or out on the town, heads will turn in admiration.

* Find the nearest orchard and pick apples. Trust me, climbing trees is still as much fun as it was when you were little.

* Jump into a huge pile of leaves.
* Carve an outrageous pumpkin and display it on your windowsill.

SPORTY

One summer a bunch of us who were lifeguards formed a softball team. And even though most of us were athletes, we were terrible. But we had a great time while we were playing and an even better time after the game!

JOIN A LEAGUE

Bowling, softball, volleyball, or tennis, it doesn't matter, and you don't have to be a superstar. Or organize a team on your own. Unless you're looking to compete seriously, recruit the most fun people, not necessarily the most athletic.

GO CHEER SOME NONPROFESSIONALS

Local high school track meets, softball games, gymnastics competitions, or swim meets don't cost much and are a great way to enjoy sports. Better yet, volunteer to help out, and you'll get involved and get in for free.

CHECK OUT YOUR COMMUNITY CENTER

A lot of these have nice facilities for you to work out in for far less than regular gym memberships. They also offer programs and leagues.

TRAIN FOR A FULL OR MINI-MARATHON

C'mon, anyone with two legs has the equipment to do it—but only the most disciplined will.

HOST THE GAME

Whether it's the Super Bowl, March Madness, the World Series, or the Indy 500, there's always a big sporting event to gather people together for and watch.

GO BOWLING

Sometimes bowling alleys have themed evenings like Disco Night, but even if they don't, make your own. Showing up with your whole posse in retro threads would be a real hoot. Or, make it "goofy bowling" and have everyone try a different maneuver each frame: wrong-handed, backwards, between your legs, between someone else's legs, on your knees, on one foot, you get the idea.

WALK, JOG, OR BIKE AT A COLLEGE CAMPUS

Even if you're not a student, you can still walk, run, or bike *around* a college campus. They're big and notoriously pretty, so you'll get plenty of exercise while enjoying the view.

KID STUFF

I have great memories of Yahtzee and root beer marathons with my brother Kyle when we were growing up. So when I recently stumbled upon a cheap, electronic Pocket Yahtzee game, I had to buy it. Yep, it's still as much fun as it was when I was a kid.

BUY A TOY FOR YOUR INNER CHILD

Scour garage sales and antique stores for that one toy you always wanted as a kid. Whether it's a specific Beanie Baby, some funky Pogs, or that Beavis and Butthead T-shirt you always wanted but your mom never let you have, you'll have fun hunting for it and even more fun haggling for it.

BE A KID IN A CANDY STORE

Sourballs, licorice, gummy worms, whatever, buy all of your favorite sweets you haven't eaten since you were little. One day of candy won't blow your diet. My friend Wendy and I conclude every shopping trip to the mall with a stop at the Mr. Bulky's candy store for a pound of our favorite candy: sourballs. We grin like schoolgirls as we happily dig into the bag and nosh.

PLAY WITH PLAYDOUGH

Squishing, molding, cutting, and creating with the soft stuff is relaxing, therapeutic, and downright fun.

LEARN A FEW GOOD MAGIC TRICKS

You can check out a book from the library and buy inexpensive magic tricks at party supply stores.

TRY OUT THE PLAYGROUND

Play hide-and-seek behind trees, go down slides, ride the merry-go-round, climb equipment, or swing on the swings as high as you can. If there's a sandbox, build castles.

ROLLER SKATE

Grab your roller-skates or rollerblades (or rent them) and head to the nearest roller rink. Be sure to try Shoot the Duck and Backwards Skate when the announcer calls them out.

HIT THE ARCADE

Check out the best entertainment that Chuck E. Cheese's has to offer. Play some video games, shoot some hoops, and enjoy a slice of pizza and beer.

CHEW BUBBLE GUM

Loudly. See how many pieces you can fit in your mouth and how big of a bubble you can blow.

RIDE A CAROUSEL

Outdoor festivals, carnivals, and amusement parks always have carousels—sometimes malls do too. Who cares if you're the biggest kid on the ride? Let your mane down.

PLAY BOARD GAMES

Clue, Monopoly, checkers, card games, Pictionary, Scrabble, Trivial Pursuit, Yahtzee, Connect Four, and more—there's probably one game that you still just love.

TRY GO-CART RACING OR PLAY MINIATURE GOLF

I don't have the patience (or the skills) to play *real* golf, but there's nothing intimidating about trying to get a ball through a windmill and into a clown's mouth.

DRAW WITH CHUBBY CHALK
Go outside and draw on the sidewalk. Don't worry— it should all wash off with a hose or when it rains next, but check the label.

TRY A HULA HOOP
It's great exercise, too.

BUY SMALL TOYS
Jacks, Pick-Up-Sticks, Etch-a-Sketches, Rubik's Cubes, and Slinkies are great to mess around with.

FAMILY

It's amazing that you can love your family so much—and that they can drive you so crazy. And even though they can embarrass you, disagree with you, and downright annoy you, they also love you, support you, and make for a lot of good times.

MAKE A DOCUMENTARY ABOUT YOUR FAMILY
Capture your little brother playing in his Pee Wee football game, your mother absentmindedly twisting her hair while pouring over a cookbook, your father tinkering (or in my case, cursing) in the garage. Be sure to narrate, and the more candid the better. Looking back on the tape someday, you'll be glad you captured these everyday rituals and habits.

CELEBRATE SOMEONE'S LIFE

Gather and display old photographs, and cruise the Internet for things that happened on that special person's birthday. Have family members write something nice or funny about the person and make the guest of honor guess who wrote what.

PUT TOGETHER A TIME CAPSULE

Cover a tin canister with contact paper and decorate it to create a commemorative piece for a newborn niece or nephew for the day she or he was born. Include a newspaper, a current fashion magazine, advertisements, an inexpensive article of clothing, family pictures, and lists of top songs, movies, books, and TV shows.

HAVE A FAMILY PORTRAIT DONE

The next time you get everyone together, have a picture taken in a beautiful outdoor setting—in a splendid garden, under the trees in fall, or by a fountain. You don't need to hire a profession-al photographer—just someone with patience and a digital cam-era so you can see if you've gotten a good shot. You only need one good picture. Have it developed into an 8" x 10" and put it in a nice frame.

TRACE YOUR FAMILY TREE

It's fascinating to learn about relatives from long ago; they're a part of your heritage. Plus you never know where a branch may lead. When I traced my family tree, I discovered that George Washington is a very, very distant relative on my great grandfa-ther's side!

WRITE A LONG LETTER
TO YOUR GRANDPARENTS

Tell them about your job, your friends, the guy you're dating—in short, tell them about your life. They want to know.

WRITE YOUR BIOGRAPHY

Since you're the author, it's up to you to decide what to include and not include.

DIRECT THE KIDS
IN A SKIT AT A FAMILY GATHERING

We once visited my Uncle Bill and Aunt Mary Ann and their seven children, and the kids put on a variety show for us (no, they're not the Von Trapp family). My cousin Jon—a natural comedian even at the age of twelve—had everyone in stitches. (Well, almost everyone—his sister Lisa was miffed that he didn't give her any of the funny lines.)

ASK YOUR PARENTS OR GRANDPARENTS
ABOUT THEIR WEDDING DAY

Where was the ceremony and reception held? What was it like? What did she wear? Who was there? Now's the time to get out the old photo albums and maybe even find Grandma's dress in the attic.

KIDNAP A FAMILY MEMBER
AND GO OUT FOR BREAKFAST

If you can do so safely, blindfold them until you reach your destination. If they have a good sense of humor, take them in their pajamas—but only if you wear yours, too.

MAKE A MOVIE

Write a script and use appropriate costumes, makeup, and venues. At the end of the day, pop a big bowl of popcorn and gather together to watch your creation.

DO SOMETHING FOR YOUR GRANDPARENTS

Take Grandma or Grandpa out to a doctor's appointment, run errands, or take them out to lunch.

HOST THE NEXT FAMILY SHINDIG

Give your mom and grandma a break from the cooking, cleaning, and entertaining. You're a big girl now and it's your turn. If you don't have the space or means to put on an elaborate spread, do a brunch buffet. Plus, now you don't have any excuse to complain about family gatherings—you can make your's however you'd like it to be.

CHARITY

Doing something for charity helps others and makes you feel good about yourself. When you support a cause, you know that you're doing something to make a difference and better the lives of others.

PARTICIPATE IN
FUNDRAISING WALKS AND RUNS

Whether it's the National Multiple Sclerosis Society's MS Walk, the Susan G. Komen Breast Foundation Race for the Cure, or a multitude of others, these walks, take place in almost every city. Most cities have local fundraising walks too. Even though a lot of these are called runs, there's always a walker's section. These walks/runs are usually held in the mornings at a local park and offer juice and breakfast foods afterward. Put a team together. You'll raise money for a good cause, spend time with friends, and get some exercise.

DONATE YOUR OLD CLOTHES

Go through your wardrobe and donate anything you haven't worn or used in over a year to the Salvation Army. You can also write it off as a tax deduction.

DONATE BLOOD

It only takes about an hour, so you can do it over lunch. Lie back and relax, enjoy some cookies and juice after you're done, and feel good knowing you may have literally helped save someone's life.

WRITE A LETTER TO A SOLDIER OVERSEAS

Tell him or her how much you appreciate them keeping you safe. Send them some candy or a mixed CD of patriotic music. Ask if they need anything sent from the States.

SPEND TIME AT THE HUMANE SOCIETY

Volunteer to help groom, walk, feed, or play with pets at an animal shelter. Offer to help clean up the cages. Bring along some inexpensive treats. You'll learn the true meaning of unconditional love.

VISIT A NURSING HOME

Spend time chatting with residents. Take them for a walk around the grounds. Play cards or checkers. Ask them about their lives and loves. Ask them for advice. They'll be grateful for the company.

VOLUNTEER AT A CHILDREN'S HOSPITAL
Read stories or play games. Better yet, rent a clown costume. Donate your old GameBoy or PlayStation and spend the day letting the kids beat you.

COACH A LITTLE LEAGUE TEAM
Teaching kids sportsmanship and skills takes time and patience, but hearing your little buddy shout, "I did it!" makes it all worthwhile.

BUY GIRL SCOUT COOKIES
Or anything else a child is selling to raise money for his or her organization. Be generous and help them get closer to their goal.

SMILE AT SOMEONE
Especially if they don't smile at you first.

TO DO! Here are events to check out around town.

....

....

....

....

....

....

What's going on in other cities that might be happening around here?

Oktoberfest in Hermann, Missouri

....

....

....

....

What parts of town haven't you explored yet?

....

....

....

....

....

TO DO! Hobbies to learn . . .

....

....

....

....

....

....

TO DO! Fun things to do in . . .

Winter

....

Spring

....

Summer

....

Fall

....

8

Look Like
a Million Bucks
(for a Lot Less)

Fashion fades, only style
remains the same.

—COCO CHANEL

WAS THRILLED WHEN MY FRIEND
MELISSA ASKED ME TO BE A BRIDES-
MAID, BUT HAVING BEEN A BRIDESMAID
seven times, I can confide that there's the moment when you brace yourself and put on a cheery face to oooh and ahhhhh for the reveal of the potential Awful Bridesmaid Dress. But when the dress for Melissa's wedding arrived, I couldn't believe it. It was beautiful. Black, sleeveless, cowl neckline, deep V in the back to the waist met by a simple tuxedo bow, and a long, slightly A-line skirt. Simple, elegant, classic, timeless, and flattering.

After the wedding my mother hemmed the dress to just above the knee because I thought I would wear it again as a cocktail dress. And I have—over and over and over. I've worn it with sheer black hose and high closed-toe heels and with high black sandals with bare legs. My accessories have ranged from my sub-dued pearl choker and earrings to colorful jewels to a beaded shawl and even a feather boa. Seven years later, I've never found another little black dress that I like better or that I think looks as good on me.

WHAT DO YOU NEED?

To figure out the kinds of clothes you need, think about your lifestyle. What kinds of things do you do? Is your profession's dress code conservative or laid-back? Do you spend your weekends curled up with a good book, browsing antique shops, rock climbing, or all of the above? Is your idea of a fun night out hanging with a small group of friends at someone's apartment, dinner and a movie, or hitting all the best clubs in town?

Your clothes will most likely fall into three categories: really casual, casual-fun, and professional/dressy. Really casual clothes are for working out, walking the dog, or lounging around the house. Casual-fun clothes are for the weekends, going out, and recreation. Professional/dressy clothes are for the office, weddings, graduations, church, showers, and so on.

These three categories will overlap, and you'll get more out of your wardrobe by mixing and matching different pieces together. Wear your jeans and that tailored blazer from your suit for a chic casual look. A sundress can be worn with high-heeled sandals and a shrug for a night out on a date, or paired with a jacket and closed-toed heels for the office, or worn with flat sandals and a sweater tied around the shoulders for a shower or brunch. This is an example of one of the golden rules of clothes-buying—versatility. The more versatile the piece, the more you'll wear it. Versatility comes from color, style, and fabric.

Dress for the occasion and for practicality. You wouldn't wear a cocktail dress to a rock concert nor would you wear your warm-up suit to a wedding. Call someone who knows the function or venue to find out the unwritten dress code. This is especially true for business after-hours parties and other related functions where first impressions are crucial. If in doubt, you'll always feel more comfortable being overdressed instead of underdressed.

PROFESSIONALLY SPEAKING

It's fine to endorse Casual Fridays if your company does. But understand there's a big difference between Corporate Casual and what you'd wear to the gym or a night out on the town. Always err on the conservative side for office attire.

Different offices have different dress codes, even if they're unwritten. A schoolteacher, accountant, and designer all work in very different environments and dress differently. Take your cue from the female higher-ups. Check your employee handbook to see if there is a written, enforced dress code.

The office is the one (and probably only!) place that you want to appear older than you are. Dress appropriately for the environment you're in and make the majority of your professional wardrobe classic, not trendy. Micro miniskirts, low-cut blouses, gigantic hoop earrings, and belly-baring tops are no-nos.

That said, your office attire doesn't have to be boring. A well-placed brooch, an interesting pendant, or a fun, printed blouse with a neutral-colored suit is fine. But limit your funky pieces. A loud color from head-to-toe is a no-go. A lime green scarf around your neck is interesting; a lime green suit makes you look like a big Skittle.

Be careful not to O.D. on the jewelry and accessories. Invest in one really nice handbag and pair of shoes in a neutral color, like black or camel, that you'll wear all the time. Trust me, it will be worth it.

As a general rule, think small and simple. A small pair of earrings, watch, ring, and the occasional bracelet is just enough, but skip the armload of bangle bracelets a la early-eighties Madonna. You want all eyes to be on your presentation, not your arm of jangling bracelets.

PUT YOUR BEST FEATURE FORWARD

I was still wearing baggy rugbys carried over from my college-style days when my then-boyfriend now-husband Jeff looked at me with that I-want-to-say-something-nice-but-I-don't-think-it-will-come-out-that-way look on his face. He said, "You're so lucky to be petite. Why do you want to add ten pounds to your frame with that oversized, shapeless shirt?" He was right, of course. (But the only time ever.)

Whether you're a size 2 or a size 22, *every* woman has great features and not-so-great ones. Not playing up your good ones and calling attention to your not-so-good ones just don't make any sense. Yes, there are a few rare genetically blessed swizzle sticks, but other than them, who doesn't want to look like they weigh five pounds less than they really do? So for the remaining 99 percent of us, here are some tried-and-true guidelines for making the most of what you've got:

Large Chest

LOOK FOR

* ✳ Wrap dresses (accentuate the waist, not the chest)
* ✳ Tasteful V-necks (highlight the goods without overemphasizing them)
* ✳ Adjustable straps (extra support)

AVOID

* ✳ Loose-fitting smock tops (appear shapeless and big all over)
* ✳ Halter necks (breasts may spill out the sides)
* ✳ Skimpy straps (too much emphasis on the chest and not enough support)

Flat Chest

LOOK FOR

* ✳ Halter (shows off shoulders)

AVOID

* ✳ Low-scoop necks (lead the eye down to, well, nothing)

Pear Shape

LOOK FOR

* A-line skirts of any length (camouflage wide hips and thighs)

* Blazers that hit just below the saddlebag spot (disguise thick thighs and make you look slightly broader at the shoulder, balancing out wide hips)

AVOID

* Cropped jackets (draw the eye immediately to the bulges)

* Pencil skirts (cling to and emphasize saddlebags)

* Pants tapered at the ankles (Making the ankles look skinnier only makes the hips look bigger.)

No Waist/Boxy

LOOK FOR

* V-necks, cinched waists (add curves where there aren't any)

AVOID

* Boat necks, sheaths (make the body look even more square)

Big Arms

LOOK FOR

* Three-quarter length sleeves (hide the flab and emphasize wrists)

AVOID

* Capped sleeves, sleeveless (show off arms)

* Spaghetti straps (Small straps make big arms look bigger.)

Junk in the Trunk

LOOK FOR

* Low-rise pants (cut the backside area in half)
* Wide-leg pants (create balance and hang away from the backside)

AVOID

* Front pleats (will be pulled out by the backside)
* Pants tapered at the ankles (make the backside look even bigger)

Tummy Pouch

LOOK FOR

* Wrap dresses (hide the folds)
* Low-waisted dress/pants (cut the stomach area in half)

AVOID

* Tight/short shirts (show off the rolls)
* Drawstring waists (add bulk where there's already enough)

Short Stature

LOOK FOR

* One strong color head-to-toe (trick the eye into seeing one long, uninterrupted line)

AVOID

* Bold print and patterned suits or dresses (break up the body and make you look shorter)

* Cutesy prints (make a petite woman look like a child)

Short Legs

LOOK FOR

* Floor-length skirts with high heels (give the illusion that it's your legs, not your shoes, that make you tall)

* Flared pants (The width of the flare covers part of the shoe, making legs seem longer.)

AVOID

* Calf-length pants or skirts (chop the leg in half, making short legs look even shorter)

Full Figure/Curvy

LOOK FOR

* Cinched waists and belts (emphasize voluptuousness)

AVOID

* Straight edges, boxy jackets (Harsh edges make curves look bigger.)

LESS IS MORE

The Paris Hiltons of the world who have a lot of clothing must get frustrated because they don't have time to wear everything, and they probably can't find what they want, or even know what they have. Having a few classic pieces that are always in style and work with each other is much better than having an entire closet jammed with the latest trends. A total wardrobe of trendy items doesn't look good for long and the pieces seldom work together.

Try to avoid filling your closet up with clothes you only wear occasionally. Let the balance of your wardrobe be the clothes you wear every day. I read somewhere that most people wear 20 percent of their clothing 80 percent of the time. Wouldn't it be better to wear 100 percent of your clothing 100 percent of the time? No lonely, forgotten pieces. Everything is used, worn out, discarded, and then replaced.

Think about buying your clothes like you buy your food. How much you are willing to spend should be determined or related to the amount of wear it will receive, like servings per box. The more times you wear

Don't Fake It

I prefer to invest in one quality, classic, real designer piece and cherish my authentic black Prada bag. It's illegal (trademark stealing) for imposters to don a real designer's label, and besides, well, it just isn't right.

Imposters have gotten so good it's often tough to tell a real from a faux. Here are some guidelines to make sure you're getting the real deal:

- The item should come with a "card" (like a small credit card) with an assigned serial number for your item and a duster (cloth sack) with the brand on it.

- Inspect details like the metal closure snap inside and the lining because most authentic pieces will have the designer's name imprinted on these and fakes won't.

- Imposters will be reduced to a ridiculously low price.

- Buy from reputable stores and check the label carefully. If you purchase it from Nordstrom's, you can be pretty sure it's the real deal; if you buy it from a guy on the street corner, you can be pretty sure it's not.

Check out eBay for quality originals from designers such as Tiffany, Cartier, Gucci, and Kate Spade. Sunglasses, purses, shoes, you name it, you can find the real goods heavily discounted. Even price clubs like Sam's and Costco carry Prada, Gucci, Fendi, and Coach purses as well as Movado, Ebel, Concord, Omega, and Cartier watches.

or use something, the cheaper it is. For example, if you live in a cold climate, your winter coat is probably worn every day. Not only is it one of the most functional pieces of clothing that you own, it almost becomes your signature piece, as some people will never see you in anything but that coat.

Make the backbone of your wardrobe one or two neutral colors that are always in style and build around that. Black, navy, white, gray, brown, and tan are great choices.

Look for items that go with anything, fit and flatter you, and are fabrics and colors that can go from season to season.

Regardless of your lifestyle, fashion tastes, and body shape, there are some basics that almost every smart wardrobe should have. Jeans, khakis, white tees and blouses, cardigan sweater sets in colors that flatter you, white pants, black pants, a long and a short black skirt, a navy or black pinstriped suit, and a little black dress are timeless wardrobe staples. Figure out the style that looks best on you and you won't look passé by the next season.

You should hang onto any piece of classic clothing that is flattering, that you like, that will get a lot of wear, is well-made, and is comfortable. The styles may alter slightly—sometimes very slightly—year to year, but you're better off buying what looks good on you, not what's trotting down the runway this fall.

Don't worry that your staples aren't "this season"—is anyone really going to notice that last year's capris hit mid-calf and this year's capris hit just below? Or that last year's hip color was celery green and this year it's spring green? And even if they do notice, do you really care?

Buy classic clothes at the end of the season when they're marked down and save them for next year. A leather coat at the end of the winter, khaki pants at the end of spring, white tees at the end of the summer. If you find something that's flattering, timeless, good quality, and it's a steal, consider buying two so you'll have a replacement on hand when the first one wears out.

Consider minimizing your accessories, too, which can get quite costly. The look you want is one of quality, not quantity. Buy the cool necklace—but skip the matching earrings and wrist cuff. And how many black belts do you really need? Too much stuff will all just get jumbled, tangled, stuffed into a drawer, and forgotten about.

PLAY FAVORITES

Everyone has favorites. A favorite color, favorite food, favorite music. And whether you're five or twenty-five, you still have a favorite outfit. It's that first thing you want to pull out of the clean laundry and wear, the first thing you reach for in your closet, the first item you can't wait to christen again when it's a new season. Because you love it and look great in it, you'll exude confidence and happiness every time you wear it.

Then there are those items that you're not quite sure about, that you keep in the back of your closet "just in case." But would you ever wear them on a job interview or a first date? Of course not. If you aren't excited to wear it, then why bother to wear it at all? Get rid of the "maybes" even if it means you have less stuff. In fact, it's probably a good thing to have less stuff. It's much better to have one great outfit than ten that are just so-so.

It's great if you can make everything in your wardrobe a favorite. Figure out exactly what it is you like about an article of clothing or an entire outfit. Is it the color? The fabric? The cut? The style? The way it feels, hangs, and the way you look in it? I didn't realize it, but every time I look for a top, I automatically look for it in a shade of spring green. Whenever I wear this color, people compliment me. Not only do I find it soothing, but I guess it's flattering on me, too. Once you figure it out what's fabulous for you, keep it in mind for all future wardrobe-building endeavors.

TRENDY WENDY

Fuchsia, ruby, magenta, hot pink, strawberry. It's funny that pretty much the same shade gets renamed each year to make it hip for that season. The fashion world tries its best to change styles and colors each year, hoping that you'll buy into the latest trends.

It's fun and fine to look hip, but keep it in check. Don't pay a lot of money for really trendy items. Check out teen shops and discount stores which offer the latest trends at inexpensive prices. The quality may not be the best, but by the time you wear them out, they'll probably be on their way out. (If you're petite, check out girl's larger clothing sizes. You'd be surprised that sometimes you can fit in them and the same garment costs less in a girl's size than an adult's. But do be careful not to select styles that are *too* young.)

Consider buying just a trendy top and pairing it with the non-trendy bottoms already in your closet. Keeping your clothes in classic lines and neutral colors on the bottom half of your body will save you money and keep you from looking too over the top. Besides, tops tend to cost less than pants or skirts, and it tends to be easier to find a better fit. Plus, putting a cool color on the top half of your body will flatter your face.

You can also make your accessories trendy instead of your clothes. Accessories cost even less than tops, and you can always find a good fit. Buy trendy accessories from teen stores like Claire's where they're less expensive than regular department stores and boutiques. Adding a fun necklace, pin, bracelet, or pair of earrings can update a tailored, classic outfit and give it instant pizzazz.

BE AN ORIGINAL

Sure, flavor-of-the-month fashion can be fun, but will your true sense of style please stand up? It's like the girl who chameleons herself according to the man she dates. You wonder, who is she *really*?

Hone your own signature style. As you go through your twenties, you'll probably gravitate more and more toward a wardrobe that's sleek, sophisticated, sexy, and uniquely you. Fashion magazines offer great guidelines, but don't put too much stock in them. Doing so might cloud your ability to decide for yourself. Pick a few timeless pieces that define you and wear them. Accessories are a great venue for this. Ask Grandma if you can dig into her costume jewelry for some fabulous originals. (For some glitz and ritz, clip her big jeweled earrings to the toes of your pumps.) Wear that one unique piece: a charm bracelet, your grandmother's brooch, a funky scarf, the gorgeous turquoise jewelry you got on your last vacation in Mexico.

I have a gold charm bracelet with a charm for every special event, hobby, vacation, or time in my life: a track shoe from my high school days as a sprinter, my college sorority lavaliere, a tiny stingray symbolizing the day I played with real ones on a vacation to Grand Cayman. These are just a few of my mementos. Not only do I have a one-of-a-kind, personalized conversation piece, but all I have to do is look down at my wrist to remember a special time.

It's easy and safe to just buy what everyone else is buying at the same stores they're buying them from and blend in. But do you really want to just blend in? You know the kind of chain stores I'm talking about. Where everyone walks out looking like carbon copies of the mannequins and each other. They're great for your basic jeans, khakis, and tees, but that alone is a little vanilla.

But you can make plain vanilla into vanilla with sprinkles on

Chicly Cheap

Here are some rules of thumb for buying cheap clothes that don't look it:

- Go for black. It hides quality indiscretions better than lighter colors and has an aura of professionalism and quality.

- Skip bright-colored leathers. There's a fine line between trendy and cheesy. Bright-colored leathers can almost look plastic. Classic shades of black and brown in leather never go out of style.

- Stick to solid-patterned jackets. Sometimes patterned jackets (e.g., pinstripes, plaids) don't line up on seams and shoulders, which is a sign of poor quality.

- Avoid shiny fabrics. They just tend to look cheap.

- Minimize the details. Reduce the number of zippers, pockets, snaps, buttons, and bows on an item. Simpler lines look cleaner.

- Choose intense hues over subdued ones. Washed-out color knits look like they're old and faded, even if they're not. Bolder hues look richer longer.

- Look for clothes with lining. They'll hold their shape better.

top. Take that basic pair of jeans, pants, blouse, purse, jacket, or shoes and embellish it. Hot glue grosgrain ribbon, fringe, beading, flowers, buttons, or jewels to the sleeves of a tee, the cuffs on your capris, the toes of your shoes, a belt, you name it. Craft and fabric stores sell rows and rows of stuff, so check them out. Loop a big ribbon through the belt loops of your pants or give form to a jacket by closing it with a brooch. You'll have that fabulous bought-it-at-a-boutique look, save money, *and* have an original.

SHOPPING SMARTS

Often when you step inside a store and the salesperson asks, "Can I help you?" it's a knee-jerk reaction to respond, "No thanks, I'm just looking." Nothing makes you feel more self-conscious than having someone watch you as you browse through racks. But sales clerks are there for another reason than to earn a commission. It's their job to help you.

Find a salesperson with a similar style or figure to yours. Communicate clearly what you're looking for and how much you want to spend. If she doesn't seem to pay attention to what you've said or doesn't seem to have your best interests at heart, move on. But if she's helpful and you're a repeat customer to a store, be sure to ask for and work with her each time.

If you see something that you really like, ask a salesperson if the item will be on sale anytime soon. Many stores have sales every weekend. Give her your business card and ask her to call you, or if she tells you when the next sale will be, jot down the date in your planner. Get there early on that date.

So what do you do if you find something that you like but they don't have your size? Almost all chain stores can call other stores in the local area; many stores also have a computer database that will allow them to check for other stores nationwide. Stores should be able to ship to other stores for free, but you'll have to go and pick your item up at your local store when it arrives.

You should rarely if ever pay full price for clothes. They'll go on sale long before the season to wear them is over. I was amazed to see all swimsuits 70 percent off at the local department store—in the middle of June. Most malls have huge "sidewalk sales" in January to clear out the merchandise left over from Christmas. So if you see something you love, try to be patient and wait for it to come on sale. Almost everything does eventually. And if that sweater you really wanted is gone, well, it just wasn't meant to be. There will be other sweaters.

But what if you buy something, whether full price or on sale, and then notice the next week that it's marked down further? If this happens within two weeks of your purchase, take the item and your receipt back to the store and most will make a price adjustment. Meaning, they'll pay you in cash the difference between your price and the sale price. This is perfectly legal, but many people don't know to ask for it.

Outlet stores and off-price apparel retailers (e.g., Marshall's, TJ Maxx, and Stein Mart) have become so popular because they offer brand names at less than department store prices. But don't be fooled into thinking that just because something is at one of these places it's automatically a bargain. Do check prices and compare them with what you've seen at department stores.

Sometimes you have to be patient and wade through things to find something you like, but if you frequent a certain one of these stores often enough, you'll develop your own efficient plan of attack. Do double-check return policies since they may not be as generous as department store's policies.

Internet shopping is also great resource. There are great deals available, you can shop any time of day, and you don't have to leave the comfort of your seat. But do proceed with caution. Here are some tips from the Federal Trade Commission to help you shop online safely:

* Use a secure browser.

* Shop with companies that you know. Anyone can set up a shop online under almost any name, so make sure you know who you're dealing with.

* Determine a company's refund and return policies *before* you place your order. These should be listed on the company's Web site.

* Keep your password private. Avoid using telephone numbers, birth dates, or parts of your Social Security number. Use a combination of letters and numbers.

* Pay with a credit or charge card. This way, your transaction is protected by the Fair Credit Billing Act, and you have the right to dispute charges under certain circumstances and withhold payment while the creditor is investigating them.

* Keep good records. Print out a copy of your purchase order and confirmation number for your files.

* Online orders are covered by the Mail and Telephone Order Merchandise Rule, which means that unless the company states otherwise, your merchandise must be delivered within thirty days; if there are delays, the company must notify you.

* Keep personal information private. Don't disclose information such as your address, telephone number, Social Security number, or e-mail address unless you know who is collecting it, why they are collecting it, and how they will use it.

* Look for an online privacy policy.

Shop for clothes only when you need, not want, something specific. Buy the item that you came in for and leave the store before you spot the cashmere sweater that would be perfect with that tweed skirt, the leather pants that would be perfect with that blouse, the boots that would be perfect with, well, everything.

While you might be tempted to buy the entire outfit off the mannequin, don't forget what you already have in your closet. Do you already have a black turtleneck or a white blouse that would go great with your newly purchased printed skirt?

I mentioned it before, but remember the rule of favorites when you're shopping: don't buy it if you don't absolutely love it. A good deal isn't a good deal if you never wear it.

Chances are, if you don't love it when it's beautifully displayed at the store, you certainly won't love it any more when you hang it at the back of your closet. You haven't saved yourself any money if you've spent money on something that probably won't be used or worn.

If you spot something that needs a minor repair—say a loose or missing button or an unraveling seam—consider how much time, money, and effort it would take you to repair it, and see if the compensation the store will give you is worth it. I was once looking for something I could wear to an annual fundraiser at the zoo and got an incredible long, sleek, sequined, zebra-patterned dress this way. It had already been marked down significantly because it was an after-prom season item in the juniors department. The zipper was a little loose at the seams, but this was an easy and cheap fix. I asked the salesperson if she could knock off 20 percent more and she did.

SECONDHAND STYLE

To get a whole new wardrobe without spending any money, have a clothes-swapping party with friends if you wear similar sizes. Even if you don't wear the same sizes, you can still exchange purses, jewelry, scarves, and other accessories. You can get rid of things that don't fit or you don't wear anymore and get some new stuff in return. One gal's trash is another gal's treasure. If there's stuff nobody wants, donate it to charity and get the tax deduction.

If it's a one-time occasion—a friend's wedding, your company's Christmas party, your niece's christening—consider borrowing something from a close friend or family member. Always dry clean something after you borrow it from someone else. Hey, dry cleaning is still a lot cheaper than buying a new outfit!

Check out thrift stores. You may have to look through a lot of stuff, but it can be well worth the hunt. Here are a few things to keep in mind when hitting secondhand stores:

CHECK AN ITEM OF CLOTHING THOROUGHLY

Look for rips, tears, stains, and missing buttons and snaps. Inspect garments carefully along the seams. Sometimes the seam isn't altogether apart, just loose, and repairing the item may be a simple enough task to justify purchasing it anyway.

LOOK FOR DEPARTMENT STORE TAGS

Sometimes thrift stores have brand-new clothes—even designer brands—with the tags still on them. Usually these items were gifts that didn't fit, couldn't be returned, or purchases that were forgotten.

GO AT THE RIGHT TIME

While people drop things off at secondhand stores all the time, there might be certain days when trucks bring in deliveries, so find out when those are. As with retail stores, hit the shops after the holidays. People tend to donate more after Christmas because they have newer clothes and other items. Spring is also a great time to look because people are doing their spring cleaning.

ALLOW YOURSELF PLENTY OF TIME TO SHOP

The more time you allow yourself to shop, the more likely you are to find a real bargain.

TO SEW OR NOT TO SEW

Sewing is a great hobby that can give you tailor-made clothes. While it can be done economically, there are some things to consider.

Sewing is a skill that has to be learned and professional finishes can be a challenge to achieve. Certain details, like embroidery, are difficult to do at home. There are also price considerations. Fabric can be expensive, and of course there is the expense of a sewing machine and other supplies.

Besides the expense of a sewing machine, there are space considerations for it as well as for cutting, ironing and an ironing board, and other supplies. Finally, when you buy clothing in the store, you immediately know how it is going to fit and look on you; when you sew something for yourself, it may not turn out like you thought it would.

On the other hand, sewing things that save you the most money and headaches makes a lot of sense. Dresses for special occasions can be difficult to find and are a good thing to make. My bridesmaids had the most diverse type of body shapes possible—tall, short, flat-chested, large-chested, pregnant, non-pregnant, you name it—and it worked out well and saved money to have their dresses tailor-made for each of them. You can almost always find patterns at 50 percent off, if not cheaper. A lot of stores will give you the pattern for free if you buy their fabric.

Even if you don't sew, do find a good, reasonably priced tailor. They're out there and they don't have to cost a fortune. I'm barely 5' 2" so I'm forever having to have pants hemmed, and finding a great tailor has proved invaluable.

HIP TIPS

Even the most gorgeous clothes look bad if they're ill-fitting, torn, wrinkled, or dirty. Here are some tips to help you look fab instead of frumpy.

* **Invest in a full-length mirror. You can buy an inexpensive one at discount stores and put it on the back of your closet door.**

* **Buy shoe polish and use it regularly on shoes, belts, and purses. It's that little detail that makes all the difference.**

* **Give yourself plenty of time if you're looking for something for a specific occasion. You don't want to feel backed into a corner and spend more than you had planned on something mediocre just because you needed *something*.**

* **Avoid Dry Clean Only clothes—dry cleaning bills week after week add up. Many clothing manufacturers are required by law to put the "safest" form of cleaning, which is often Dry Clean Only. Sometimes garments can be hand washed in cold water even if the tag says Dry Clean Only, so check. You can usually hand wash your sweaters instead of sending them to the dry cleaner.**

* **Buy low-maintenance, high-wear fabrics. A rayon-polyester blend is a great one. It can go from one season to the next, doesn't require ironing (unless it's crumpled in the bottom of your closet), and cleans easily.**

* If you do buy a fabric that wrinkles easily like linen, there's no way around it—you gotta iron it. Allow plenty of time to iron a piece before you intend to wear it. Keep a can of spray starch on hand and use it to make your ironed clothes look crisp.

* Comfort and a good fit are the key. You don't want to be adjusting your bra strap, picking your underwear out of your crack, or hobbling around in shoes that hurt. If something fits right and is made for you, you shouldn't have to fiddle with it. It's good for clothes to be fitted; it's bad for them to be tight.

* Buy in bulk. You'll always need more trouser socks, athletic socks, and pantyhose, so buy them ahead and in six-pack pairs if you can.

Reality check: What are your best features? What are your worst features? What colors, cuts, and styles look best on you? (Ask a painfully honest friend if you need help answering these questions.)

....

....

....

....

Maybe it's time to redefine your style. What do you have too much of? What do you need more of?

....

....

....

....

....

TO DO! Three essential wardrobe staples you should get . . .

....

....

....

....

....

TO DO! Get rid of your "maybes."

....

....

....

....

....

These shops are your favorite places to pick up groovy pants, tops, purses, and here's why . . . (an idea generator for future shopping excursions)

....

....

....

....

....

Do you have any major occasions this year that you can shop ahead for and wear more than once using different accessories? (Don't forget about rehearsal dinners, weddings, graduations, big parties, first-meeting-of-his-parents.)

....

....

....

9

Health and Beauty

Even I don't wake up looking like
Cindy Crawford.

—CINDY CRAWFORD

IT WAS IN HIGH SCHOOL THAT I FIRST FELL IN LOVE. WITH A SHADE OF LIPSTICK KNOWN SIMPLY AS BLACKBERRY. We were on and off for a few years, but we always got back together. I did see other lipsticks—Cabernet Cabaret, Bordeaux, Raisin Rage—but it just didn't work out. Blackberry always looked good on me, no matter the time of day, season, or occasion. It enhanced the natural shade of my lips, made my eyes sparkle, and made my skin glow. People have asked me for, well, a lot of years, what the shade is, and thank goodness it continues to be made.

We're still happily together today.

DON'T TEAR YOUR HAIR OUT!

Every woman wants to look good but beauty products and services are a big chunk of change for most of us. Manicures, pedicures, haircuts, color, waxing, spa treatments, products, tools, cosmetics—it adds up. But maybe there's *somewhere* that you can cut back. Think about the services and products you really value and those you can deep-six. If you want to get your hair highlighted at the salon, can you give yourself manis at home? When it comes to your hair, do you really need sculpting gel, mousse, styling lotion, cream, volumizing spray, foam, anti-frizz cream, hairspray, hair spritz, light conditioning treatment, medium conditioning treatment, deep conditioning treatment, and so on and so forth?

Perhaps you can get a good haircut from a stylist two or three times a year and use cheaper places for in-between maintenance. Better yet, opt for a style that requires little maintenance. If you grow out the layers in your hair you'll need far fewer trims. Even if you opt for a low-maintenance hairstyle, you'll want to keep your ends nice and neat. Scraggly split ends are just plain

Natural Woman

For a great deep hair conditioning treatment at home, all you need is an avocado, heavy cream, and honey. Remove the skin from one avocado and cut it into chunks. Mix it in a blender with two tablespoons of heavy cream and one tablespoon of honey. Comb the mixture through freshly washed hair. Wrap your head with a plastic grocery bag and cover the bag with a towel. Let it sit for fifteen minutes and rinse well. The fats in the avocado and heavy cream are rich in emollients that quickly penetrate the hair. They honey prevents the scalp from being too dry or too oily and is also a natural antibacterial.

unattractive, but fortunately it's not expensive to get them trimmed. Or learn how to trim them yourself—it's not too hard.

If your haircut or color is fairly simple or if you don't want something drastic, consider trying a beauty school. You'll get a trained student practicing under the watchful eye of an instructor for a very cheap price.

If you can, try and schedule your hair appointment during the week when it's not as busy. Your hairdresser will be able to make more time for you than on a Saturday afternoon, and they might even offer discounts or specials.

Take pictures of hairstyles and color with you. Your idea of chestnut honey brown may be very different than your stylist's, so *show* her what you mean. Even though your hair may be very different than the model or celebrity's in the magazine, it will at least give your stylist an idea of what you want. She isn't a mind reader.

If you get a cut or color that makes you do cartwheels, take a photo of it and bring it with you for future cuts and colors. Pay attention to the tools and techniques your stylist uses—how she handles your hair, the products and amounts of them she uses, how she angles the dryer—so that you can copy them at home. Investing in a powerful hairdryer (at least 1,875 watts and two settings) that's strong enough to manipulate your hair is the key to a good blowout.

Whether or not you get professional color or do it yourself, you have to stay on top of root growth. If you can't afford to keep up with your color, stick to your natural color. Even if you're clad from head to toe in Prada, nothing makes a woman look cheaper than an inch of dark roots sprouting from her scalp.

If you want to try coloring your own hair, proceed with caution. Semi-permanent color is the best foolproof at-home color for beginners because there are no caps, applicators, wands, or brushes—you just shampoo it in. Since it's low in peroxide, it's not damaging and the color fades in six weeks. For the best at-home color, go only one or two shades lighter than your *real* color. Read and follow the directions exactly, and don't skip the all-important strand test. Relax and focus on the task at hand—don't try to also cook dinner while you're coloring. Be obsessive about the processing time—set an alarm if you have to. Feel free to call the telephone number enclosed in the kit if you have any questions.

If you just want to boost your natural color, well, naturally, here's some hue help:

✳ BLONDES
Fill a spritz bottle with one cup of strongly brewed, cooled chamomile tea. Mist it all over clean, damp hair. Leave on for twenty minutes and then rinse and shampoo.

✳ BRUNETTES
Pour a cup of lukewarm coffee (your choice on the flavor!) over damp hair. Let it soak in for thirty minutes, rinse, and shampoo.

✳ REDHEADS
Mix a half cup of beet juice and a half cup of carrot juice. Pour it over damp hair and leave on for one hour. Rinse and shampoo. Repeat daily until you reach your desired color.

If your hair is long, for a sleek, classic look, part hair on one side, smooth back, and secure it low at the neck with a ponytail elastic. Pull some strands out of the underneath part of the ponytail and wrap them around the elastic band so that that elastic does not show, and bobby pin underneath. If your hair is shorter, opt for a far side part and secure hair to one side with a fancy barrette or bobby pin, or bobby pin in a fresh flower for a festive look.

If you want an easy, instant glamorous look for your hair or you're having a bad-hair day, invest in a small hairpiece that attaches with a comb (one clever guy I know calls it a "wiglet"). You can get them in varying lengths and colors at beauty warehouses for about $20. Find one that matches the closest to your hair when pulled back. (If your hair color tends to yo-yo quite a bit from dark to light, you might want to invest in two.) Simply pull all of your hair back into a ponytail, secure with an elastic, and clip the wiglet on top. Or, pull just a section back, secure with a small hair clip, and affix the wiglet on top of that.

FACE IT

You don't need expensive cleansers or a twenty-step program to have a clean face and clear skin. A lot of dermatologists I know recommend Dove soap as the best cleansing agent, and at around 59¢ a bar, it's a steal. I've used it for years. Cetaphil Gentle Skin Cleanser is another good one, but it can be more expensive.

It's easy to be unsure of exactly what type of skin you have. Maybe you think your skin is dry, but really you've overcleansed it and stripped it of its natural oils. To assess your skin's true state, try a simple blot test in the afternoon. Gently press a tissue onto your face. If it sticks to your whole face and you can see oil on it, you have oily skin. If it's oily in the T-zone, you have combination skin. If it doesn't stick at all, you have normal skin, unless you see flakes, in which case it's dry.

Whatever your complexion, you can enhance it with this concoction: Mash half of a ripe banana and apply it over your face

Double Duty Beauty Booty

You might know the main use for the cheap products below, but you might be surprised at what else they can do.

WITCH HAZEL–This soothing, refreshing, and mild liquid is the base ingredient for many health and beauty care products. It's a great astringent for your skin and is also good for insect bites, minor scrapes and cuts, and windburn.

EPSOM SALTS–Made of the mineral magnesium sulfate, when the salts are absorbed through the skin (such as in a bath) they draw toxins from the body, sedate the nervous system, reduce swelling, and relax muscles. They're also a great exfoliator.

BABY WIPES–Great for removing eye makeup.

VASELINE–Removes makeup, heals really dry skin, and gives lips a hint of gloss.

ANTIBACTERIAL HAND SOAP–If you discover your deodorant has expired, rub a bit of this under your arms. It kills the bacteria that causes body odor and neutralizes any odor.

ALOE–Great for dry and itchy skin as well as mild burns and sunburn. Some preliminary medical studies show that it may also boost the immune system and help treat certain kinds of cancer and diabetes.

BIG, COARSE EMORY BOARDS–Typically used to file acrylic nails, these are great for removing the really tough skin on your heels and balls of your feet.

HAND LOTION–Use a pea-sized amount, rub your hands together, and run your fingers through your hair to tame frizzies and split ends.

BAKING SODA–Can be used as an antacid (when thoroughly dissolved) and to brush your teeth.

and neck with your fingertips. Leave it on for fifteen minutes and rinse with lukewarm water. (Banana contains phosphorus, an element that brings about a natural, healthy glow.)

SAVE FACE

The best way to fix wrinkles on your face is to prevent them. The great thing is, if you're in your twenties, you can greatly reduce wrinkles if you start *now*. Always, always use a sunscreen on your face, don't smoke, and drink plenty of water to help skin keep its elasticity. These are much cheaper and painless alternatives to Botox injections, chemical peels, or (yikes!) plastic surgery.

PERK UP YOUR PEEPERS

Whether you were up late preparing for a big presentation, out on the town, or enjoying a late-night rendezvous, there are going to be times when you're just plain pooped. It will show on your face, particularly your eyes. To soothe tired eyes, put a slice of cucumber, a cold used teabag, or a cotton ball soaked in cold milk over each eye and sit back and relax for a few minutes. Minimizing your salt and liquid intake (except water) will also help reduce the puffiness.

MAKEUP, NOT MADE-UP

Makeup should be pretty but understated. It's best when someone can't even tell if you have it on. The most chic look is sheer foundation, mascara, neutral eye shadow, peachy blush, and rosy lip gloss. And never, ever go to bed with your makeup on, no matter how tired you are. It's just so bad for your skin. Always wash your face at night.

If you stick with neutral hues you can wear them year round. You can always change your look with just your lipstick, like deeper colors in the fall and paler shades in the spring, and a good nude or pink is always in style.

If you're not sure what makeup you should use, visit the makeup counter at the department store and find a sales clerk whose makeup you like. Don't feel pressured into buying everything she puts on you or think that you need every piece of the program. After all, her job is to sell you stuff. But it will give you an idea of the colors you should look for, and do buy that one product that she used on you that you love.

Good Scents for No Cents

The next time you're thumbing through your fave women's magazines, tear out and save any of the flaps of perfume samples that you like. These are perfect for a one-time application, plus you may just stumble upon your new signature scent. Store them in Ziploc snack bags (or anything that seals well).

EYEBROW WOW

I think we women as a species tend to over-tweeze our eyebrows because the thought of resembling a Cro-Magnon makes us cringe. But surprisingly, most women make the mistake of getting them a little too thin. Let your eyebrows grow out and have them professionally waxed once or twice a year. This will give you the basic shape that you need, and you can then keep up with them by tweezing the hairs that grow in. If your brows need some filling in, skip "painting" or "drawing" them in. Instead, try gently "dotting" the sparse spots with a small stiff brush and a brown eye shadow that matches or is slightly lighter than your brow hair.

Sweet Lips

Here is a delicious and inexpensive recipe for making your own lip gloss at home:

- 1 teaspoon Crystal Light fruit-flavored drink or lemonade powder in your choice of flavor*

- water

- red food coloring (optional)

- 1 tablespoon of petroleum jelly

- small container (i.e., craft case, contact lens case, plastic pill case)

Put the teaspoon of Crystal Light powder in a small dish and add 2-3 drops of water. Mixture will be thick—you want just enough water to dissolve the crystals.

Once crystals are completely dissolved, add a drop or two of food coloring if you like and stir with a spoon. Put the petroleum jelly in a separate dish and microwave it until it liquifies. Once liquefied, add the Crystal Light mixture. Stir until well mixed and pour immediately into container. Allow contents to set about half an hour before using.

*The flavored powder must be sugar-free. If the lip gloss has sugar in it, it will be too sticky.

LIP SERVICE

It's easy for your lips to get dry because they're exposed to the elements. It's a natural habit to lick your lips, which only makes things worse. Take a warm washcloth and gently rub lips to exfoliate the dead flakes. Or, try this yummy exfoliating concoction: Squeeze enough juice from an orange so that when mixed with one tablespoon of brown sugar it forms a paste. (Oranges contain acids that help shed dead skin and sugar grains are great natural exfoliators.) Use circular movements to rub the mixture gently on your lips for a few minutes with your fingers. Wash off the sugar mixture and apply Vaseline while your lips are still damp to seal in moisture.

When it comes to choosing lip color, go lighter. Ultimately the most natural color is your own and it's pretty just as it is slicked up with just a touch of Vaseline. If you want more color, stick to sheer pinks or beiges. You don't need day lipsticks and evening lipsticks. If you find a hue that looks good on you, use it all the time. Slick on some Vaseline before applying it during the day so that the color will be more sheer. At night, apply a thicker layer of lipstick for more intense color.

GIVE 'EM A HAND

No matter how tired, busy, or stressed you are, try to always keep your nails looking nice. It's that little extra detail that goes a long way. Clip and file your nails, push your cuticles back, and apply a clear or sheer polish. If your nails tend to be weak, apply a hardener or fortifier until they strengthen.

If you're a nail-biter—and I was for years—stop it *now*. It's just not something a grown woman should do. Neither the act of nibbling nor the end result is a pretty sight. Paint your nails, chew gum, sit on your hands, or do whatever you have to do to stop.

Doing your own nails will not only save you money, but it can be a very relaxing ritual. Or, you can have a Girl's Night with a friend and do each other's nails. With all the money you're saving, you can afford to splurge on a good but inexpensive wine (see chapter 6 for some suggestions) to enjoy while you're giving each other manicures—and a lot of nail salons don't offer that!

For the perfect manicure, start off with a five-minute hand massage with hand lotion which will penetrate the skin and soften cuticles. Use an orange stick to gently push back cuticles. Clip each nail once straight across and so that all nails are the same length. Use a large, very fine nail file and, holding it parallel to your finger, file upward so that the top of the nail and the nail file form a 90 degree angle. Then, file the edges of the two corners on top however square, round, oval, or "squoval" that you want.

Roll your bottle of fingernail polish between your palms for a few minutes to blend the color (don't shake—it can create bubbles). Apply a base coat and then one to two coats of your favorite polish followed by a clear topcoat. For the most classic look, stick with sheer nudes. For olive skin, choose pale pink polishes, and for pinker skin, choose a pale beige. Clear polish is always a good choice.

Nothing is more clean looking than a French manicure, and with just a little practice, you can have your nails looking salon perfect. You can buy a French manicure kit at the drugstore, or you can buy a white nail polish and a pale pink or beige one. I like my nails to be a very sheer pink with white tips, so I start with a basecoat followed by one coat of pale pink polish. After that dries, I quickly swipe the white polish once across the nail tip from left to right. Then I seal it with a topcoat.

Moisturize your hands and cuticles with lotion from time to time while you watch TV. Not only is this relaxing, but it will help strengthen your nails and moisturize dry cuticles to cut down on hangnails. For a terrific deep moisturizing overnight treatment, cover your hands in Vaseline, slip on some rubber gloves, and catch your zzzzzz's.

To help keep your nails healthy, wear rubber gloves if possible when immersing your hands in water. You'd probably be surprised to realize how much of the time your hands spend in water, which weakens your nails. Keep emery boards in your purse, desk, medicine cabinet, and car to repair any nail damage right away.

Cosmetics Clean-Up

It's not just that it's annoying having to scrape the bottom of your lipstick tube, it's unsanitary too. Makeup is a feeding frenzy for bacteria and infections can easily be spread through it. You can also avoid this by not sharing makeup with friends, sharpening pencils frequently to remove dirty outer layers, using disposable makeup sponges, and keeping makeup tightly closed and stored in a cool place.

Here's a rule of thumb for when to toss your stash in the trash:

MASCARA: 3–6 months

EYE PENCILS: 3–6 months

EYE SHADOW: 8–12 months

CONCEALER: 8–12 months

FOUNDATION: 6–12 months

LOOSE/PRESSED POWDER: 8–12 months

BLUSH: 8–12 months

LIPSTICK: 6–12 months

While you're at it, don't forget to clean your beauty tools too. Wash makeup brushes and hairbrushes with a mild shampoo every few months, and snip any frayed ends of your makeup brushes with a manicure scissors so blush goes on without streaking. Clean out the filter of your hairdryer with a toothbrush.

PAMPER YOUR PIGGIES

That grueling Pilates workout, shopping until you drop, stepping out in your favorite stilettos. It all takes a toll on your tootsies and your body as a whole. But you can rejuvenate them with a simple self foot massage.

Sit on a chair and place one foot on the opposite thigh. Rub some massage oil or lotion onto your foot if you like. Apply pressure with your thumbs to the sole of your foot, working from the bottom of your arch to the top near your big toe and repeat five times. Then, make a fist and press your knuckles into the bottom of your foot, moving from your heel to your toes and repeat five times.

Massage each toe by holding it firmly between two fingers and twisting it gently from side to side. Hold your toes in one hand and bend them backward holding them there for five to ten seconds. Then bend them in the opposite direction and hold for five to ten seconds. Repeat three times. Press and roll your thumbs between the bones of the ball of your foot. After you've done this on one foot, switch feet and repeat. You can also pamper your piggies by soaking them in a tub of warm water with a cup or two of Epsom salts.

Really rough dead skin is a challenge for most people's feet. The skin on my heels and balls of my feet can get so tough that I've found a large coarse emery board works even better than a pumice stone. Don't forget about other parts of your body that get rough too, such as elbows, heels, and knees. Loofah these

areas while in the shower and, after you get out, pat dry and
apply lotion immediately all over your body to seal in moisture.
Avoid really hot water which tends to dry skin out.

After you've soaked and exfoliated your feet, slather Vaseline
on them and wrap them in plastic wrap. Then wrap a hot towel
over each foot and kick back, or if you need to walk around,
nuke a pair of thin cotton socks in the microwave for a few seconds and slip them on over the plastic wrap. Wear for an hour,
rinse off, and apply your regular moisturizer.

To get a pretty pedicure, follow the same procedure for the
manicure above but use a toenail clipper instead of a fingernail
clipper. Wedge spacers in between your toes while you paint to
keep them from smudging.

IS THERE A DOCTOR IN THE HOUSE?

Chapter 10 will give you the skinny on health insurance, but
regardless of your plan you'll need to choose a primary care
physician for overall medical care. It could be a family practitioner, general practitioner, internist, or obstetrician/gynecolo-
gist. When you need a specialist (such as a dermatologist), your
primary care physician can refer you to one. Some specialists
will not accept patients unless referred by a primary care physician and some insurance companies will not pay for specialist's
care without a prior referral.

In some managed care plans, you will have to choose a doctor from a list of doctors in your plan; in other plans, some

doctors may be "preferred," which means they are part of a network and you will pay less if you use them. Ask your plan for a list or directory of providers, as this is also a good starting point for finding a doctor. Doctors go in and out of systems, so be sure to check every single time that you go to your chosen doctor that he or she is still in your plan.

The best time to find a doctor is before you need one. In fact, some health insurance policies require you to list one when you sign up, so you'll need to find one pronto. Ask friends, family, coworkers, and doctors you know for recommendations. Local medical societies usually have a physician referral service and will give you names based on your geographical area or the type of physician you need. If you've just moved, your former physician, may be able to recommend someone in your new area. When considering a physician, keep in mind the geographic location of their office and associated hospitals with proximity to your work and home.

Before you choose a physician, call and make an appointment to meet with him or her. It is best to meet when there is nothing urgently wrong and you are not acutely ill. This meeting will give you an opportunity to determine whether you are comfortable with the physician, the support staff, and the facilities. (Sometimes doctor's offices and hospitals have open houses when potential patients can meet doctors.) If you do make an appointment with a doctor, be prepared to discuss any special concerns or needs you have, and be prepared to pay for the office visit.

Here are some questions to ask a potential new doctor:

✳ **Are you accepting new patients?**

✳ **Which insurance plans do you accept?**

✳ At which hospitals do you have staff privileges and admit patients?

✳ Are there any limitations to your privileges?

✳ Do you practice alone, or are you part of a group?

✳ If so, how many members are there in your group?

✳ Who provides care for your patients in your absence?

✳ Are you certified by a medical specialty board? Which one? In what specialty area? (Although all doctors must be licensed to practice medicine, some are also board certified, which means the doctor has completed several years of training in a specialty and passed an exam.)

After your appointment, think about your initial impression of the doctor, staff, and facility, your satisfaction with the doctor's answers, and the way that you were treated. After you have chosen a doctor, be sure to let your plan administrator know. If at any time you are no longer comfortable with your doctor, you can usually choose another one. Just be sure to check with your plan administrator first and let her know in writing of the change so she can note it.

Checkup Checklist

Most health insurance plans cover at least one free exam a year, so check with yours to see what preventative services it offers. If you're between the ages of twenty and thirty-five, here are the general guidelines for whom to see and what to have done when. But if you have problems or a family history of something, your doctor may want to see you more often.

✔ Twice yearly dental exams and cleanings

✔ Annual pap smear, pelvic, and breast exam (plus monthly self-breast exams)

✔ Blood pressure every two years

✔ Annual vision exam

✔ Baseline cholesterol screening every five years

✔ Skin cancer examination (frequency dependent upon skin type, family history, sun exposure, and moles) plus monthly self-exams

HEALTHY HABITS

Nothing can replace the importance of regular checkups with health care practitioners (see the sidebar for checkup guidelines), but there are some easy, important things you can do to safeguard your health.

TAKE A DAILY MULTIVITAMIN MADE ESPECIALLY FOR WOMEN

Men and women have different needs, so a multivitamin made for women is the best bet. Vitamins aren't a replacement for good nutrition, but they do help balance out any deficiencies from less than stellar eating habits. The nutrition they provide helps people feel better, have more energy, ward off illness, and assist the body with normal functions. All women of childbearing age who are sexually active should be sure to take a vitamin with folic acid to prevent neural tube defects in the event that they become pregnant.

FLOSS

Daily flossing removes bacteria from teeth and gums and diminishes your chances of gum disease. Medical research shows it may also help reduce your chances of heart disease, diabetes, and respiratory disease.

EXERCISE REGULARLY

A brisk thirty-minute walk three or four times a week is good for your body and soul. If you're having difficulty making it happen, try taking the stairs instead of elevators, parking your car a little farther away, walking to do your errands, or jumping rope in your livingroom.

GET ENOUGH SLEEP

The average adult needs seven to eight hours of sleep a night so that the mind and body can function normally. Of course, there will be times when you get less than that, and that's fine from time to time. But routinely getting less than that can put you into "sleep debt" and lower your resistance and reduce your ability to perform daily routines and activities. More seriously, sleep deprivation is a leading cause of accidents behind the wheel.

WEAR SUNSCREEN

I admit it. In my teens, I was a lifeguard, a sun worshipper, and hit the tanning bed a few times before special occasions. Fortunately, I decided to save my skin in my early twenties before it was too late, and now I slather on the

Medicine Cabinet Essentials

There's nothing worse than waking up in the middle of the night with an upset tummy—and nothing in your place to soothe it. If allergy season is just around the corner and it hits you hard every year, get your refill ready or make an appointment with your allergist. Most of these medicines have a fairly long shelf life, but do check the expiration dates from time to time. Here are some things to keep stocked in your medicine cabinet:

- Pain relievers like Tylenol, aspirin, ibuprofen, and Midol
- Cold and flu medicine like Tylenol Cold
- Cough syrup and cough or zinc lozenges
- Vicks vapor rub
- Pepto Bismol
- Laxatives
- Bag of frozen peas in the freezer as an ice bag
- Assortment of band aids and bandages
- Neosporin
- Rubbing alcohol and hydrogen peroxide
- Tweezers, needles, and small scissors
- Nail clippers and emery boards
- Cotton balls and cotton swabs
- Tampons and pads
- Vaseline
- Condoms, if you're sexually active

If you don't have an aloe vera plant in your kitchen, consider putting one in your bathroom. Besides a pretty plant, you can snap off a stalk and rub it on your skin to soothe mild burns, dry skin, and sunburn.

sunscreen when I'm outside and stay out of the tanning beds. It's been scientifically proven that sunscreen reduces the risk of sunburns, premature aging, skin damage, and most importantly, skin cancer.

Of course, your skin type and family history play an important part in your risk factors as well. The majority of sun damage occurs in childhood and early adulthood, but it's not too late to start saving your skin *now*. Wear sunscreen every time your skin is exposed to harmful rays, not just when you're in a swimsuit. Pay careful attention to those areas that get a lot of exposure, like your nose, shoulders, the tips of your ears, and the tops of your legs and arms. Also, a lot of moisturizers and cosmetics contain sunscreen, so look for those. Forgo the tanning bed, too. If you want a golden glow, there are now a lot of great sunless tanning products and bronzers on the market, so experiment with them.

Keep an eye on your existing moles and be on the lookout for any new ones. A normal mole is solid tan, brown, dark brown, or flesh-colored. Its edges are well-defined. It's usually smaller than 1/4 inch in diameter and has a round or oval shape. It should be flat or dome-like. If you notice anything suspicious, see your doctor right away.

PERFORM A MONTHLY SELF-BREAST EXAM

Examining your breasts every month, along with an annual exam by your doctor, is a critical way to detect breast cancer early when it's most likely to be cured. Ask your doctor to show you how to do one. A good time to check is when you're in the shower and your skin is slick, and you can even get a free self-breast exam shower card from your doctor to remind you.

EAT A BALANCED DIET

It's important to eat well to maintain a healthy weight, fight disease, and allow your body and mind to function as they should. Regardless of how closely you count your calories or carbs, you need good nutrition. Eating a variety of good foods—including plenty of vegetables, fruit, protein, calcium, and grain products—while watching fats and sugars will help you get the energy, protein, vitamins, minerals, and fiber you need for good health. Your skin, hair, nails, and even your eyes (not to mention your insides!) reflect whether or not you're eating well.

DRINK MILK

Milk is a great source of protein and calcium for healthy teeth and bones. Bones continue to grow and are at their strongest while you are in your twenties, and they start to weaken in the mid-thirties. Even though you're a long way from menopause (usual onset age is forty-five to fifty-five), this is when osteoporosis can begin to set in due to lower levels of estrogen, which keeps bones strong. If you can't drink milk, find other sources to get your fill of calcium.

WASH YOUR HANDS FREQUENTLY

Use paper towels instead of cloth when possible to reduce the spread of germs. Keep a small bottle of antibacterial hand soap in your purse, desk, and car.

DRINK WATER

Nearly every function of the body is linked to the flow of water through your system. Water carries nutrients to vital organs, helps keep your body cool in extreme heat, aids in weight maintenance, quenches your thirst better than anything else, hydrates your skin, has zero calories, and is free. Drinking plenty of water can also help reduce your chances of urinary tract infections, which are very common in women due to the way our bodies are built. If you get bored with plain ol' agua, add a slice of lemon, lime, some raspberries, or blueberries to give it just a hint of flavor.

STOCKING UP

If you have the storage space (under your bed is just fine), stock up on toiletries such as shampoo, deodorant, toothpaste, soap, ibuprofen, etc., in bulk from volume-discount stores. You'd be surprised at how many salon brands are now sold at discount stores and wholesale clubs. Beauty warehouses are another great option if you can't find your particular brand at a volume-discount store. You'll save money and time not having to make a dash to the grocery store when you run out of toilet paper.

Compare the ingredients on store brands and name brands for shampoos, face creams, and lotions. They're often the same or very similar, but store brands cost much less. If there is a particular toiletry, hair care product, or cosmetic that you just love, go to the product's Web site and see if you can download a coupon for it.

When it comes to medicines or prescriptions from your doctor, ask for free samples. Pharmaceutical companies flood doctors with all kinds of samples of expensive prescriptions. If your doctor doesn't offer, ask. If he does write you a prescription, ask if there is a generic brand available that will work.

CHEAT SHEET! What tricks of the makeup trade do you use all the time?

Do your girlfriends have any you can try out?

....

....

....

....

What beauty products would prompt you to start a letter-writing campaign if
they were discontinued?

....

....

....

....

What products have you bought that promised things they didn't deliver?
Keep tabs on them here—and don't fall for it again!

....

....

....

....

....

Homemade beauty remedies

Homemade health remedies

TO DO! This year, I plan to . . .

Floss every day

....

....

....

....

....

....

....

....

....

10

Expecting
the Unexpected

Life is what happens when
you're busy making other plans.

—JOHN LENNON

I WAS SITTING AT MY DESK TYPING UP A PRESS RELEASE WHEN BAM! IT HIT ME. THE MOST INTENSE, SEARING PAIN IN MY lower left side. It took my breath away. One trip to the emergency room and several doses of Demerol later, I learned that I'd had a kidney stone. (For those of you who have heard a kidney stone is as bad as giving birth, I've done both and can set the record straight: childbirth was a cakewalk in comparison). It was a little unsettling a few weeks later when the hospital bills and charges for that one incident came rolling in. But fortunately, I had good health insurance through my employer *and* a good idea of how it worked.

No one plans on having a kidney stone, car accident, or losing their job, but bleep happens. Preparing for some of life's unplanned events *and* knowing what to do after something happens will help keep your stress level from kicking into overdrive. Hopefully you've stuck to your budgeting and put away money in your emergency fund (see chapter 2) in case you have out-of-pocket medical expenses, car repairs, a job loss, or other unforeseen circumstances.

Never, ever, *ever* go without health insurance, car insurance, or renter's insurance. Not having insurance is a surefire way to get yourself heavily into debt quickly, and you may find yourself (literally) paying for it for the rest of your life. Forgo buying another sweater at Barney's each month to make the small monthly payments for insurance premiums—it will be worth it in the long run.

HEALTH INSURANCE

The point of having health insurance is to keep you and your family from shelling out big bucks in case of a major medical emergency and/or chronic illness. As the story at the beginning of this chapter illustrates, illness or injury can happen to anyone at any time. Even though it might seem like you're getting a bum deal—I mean, you pay a premium each month whether or not you use it, you may have to meet a deductible before your insurance kicks in, you may pay a copay or coinsurance and pay for prescriptions, and you may have some out-of-pocket expenses —it's still pennies compared to if you had to pay for an entire medical procedure all by yourself. Paying a couple of hundred or even a couple of thousand dollars a year is a lot less than paying a couple of hundred thousand dollars. If you can't pay your medical bills, you'll have those pesky bill collectors hounding you until you do pay. If you still can't pay, you'll be faced with a lawsuit, and then you'll be faced with personal bankruptcy which will wipe out your credit for several years. You won't be able to get credit cards or loans to buy a house or a car. Talk about hitting rock bottom.

It's usually cheapest to use the health insurance offered by your employer because they pay a portion of your premium; if you look for health insurance coverage on your own, you're *on* your own to pay for all of it. Know the skinny on how your health insurance policy works, and if you don't understand something, ask your Human Resources or your benefits provider—that's their job. The healthcare industry is always changing, but it's your job to keep up with it. If in doubt, make a call before you receive any services. You'd hate to go to a doctor or hospital who isn't in your system or not get the proper preauthorization for a service and be denied coverage—and end up paying for it all out of your own pocket.

It's best to know what to do before you're faced with a medical emergency (and no, a hangnail doesn't count). It's not good to wait until you're doubled over in pain from appendicitis to figure out what hospital you should go to and where it's located. Here are some questions to ask about your health insurance policy *before* you have to use it:

* **Do I need to choose my primary care physician from a certain list, or can I go to anyone?**
* **Who are the doctors and hospitals in my healthcare system?**
* **Do I need a referral from my primary care physician before I see a specialist?**
* **Where is the nearest hospital in my system?**
* **What do I need to do if I'm hurt badly out of town?**
* **What is my monthly premium?**
* **What preventative services are included?**

Glossary of Health Insurance Terms

ALLOWABLE COSTS–Covered costs of a medical insurance plan.

(PRIOR) AUTHORIZATION–If a physician wants to perform a surgery, order a medical supply, or refer the patient to a specialist, an authorization and approval by the health plan is required.

BENEFIT LEVELS–The most that a person can receive for a service or procedure under a policy.

CLAIM– A request for payment by a medical provider for a given medical service or item. Often, the doctor's office or hospital will submit a claim to your insurance, but ask.

COPAY–The portion of a bill that you pay, usually at the time of service. It's often a set fee for a specific service.

DEDUCTIBLE–A set dollar amount which must be met during a specific time frame before the health plan begins making payments on your claims.

ENROLLMENT PERIOD–The time period during which you can join a health plan.

EXPLANATION OF BENEFITS (EOB)–Paperwork sent by your insurer to you listing the cost of treatment, the charges paid by the plan, and the remainder to be paid by you. This is not a bill

OUT-OF-POCKET EXPENSE–The amount you have to pay because it's not paid for by the insurance plan.

OUT-OF-POCKET MAXIMUM–Limit per year you'll have to pay out-of-pocket before your insurance company compensates for 100 percent of your health care costs. It includes things like deductibles, coinsurance, and copayments, and it's especially important in case of serious illness.

PREEXISTING CONDITION–A medical condition diagnosed before the effective date of your health plan that may not be covered by your plan.

PREMIUM–The fee you pay to be covered by your health insurance company, which is a set amount, usually paid each month. (If you're insured through your employer, the money will be taken out of your paycheck each month with your other withholdings so you'll never miss it.)

* Do I have a yearly deductible? What is it?

* Do I have a copay? How much is it?

* What are my yearly maximum allowed benefits?

* What is the cost of generic and brand prescription drugs?

* Do I need prior authorization for certain procedures?

* Is vision and/or dental and any other "extra" coverage included?

Your insurance will probably fall into one of two of the most common types of managed health care systems: the Health Maintenance Organization (HMO) or Preferred Provider Organization (PPO). HMO members have to choose a primary care physician (PCP) from among the HMO member physicians. The primary care physician provides general medical care and must give the okey-dokey before you can see a specialist, who must also be part of the HMO. HMOs do not tend to provide coverage for care received from doctors out of your system (with exceptions for emergency care while out of town). HMOs typically do not set deductibles that have to be met before your insurance benefits begin. Instead, HMO members often pay a small copayment for care.

PPO members do not choose a primary care physician and can go to any specialists they'd like. PPO members are not required to stay within the PPO network, but there is usually a big financial incentive to do so. For example, the PPO may reimburse 90 percent of your costs for care received within the network, but only 70 percent of your costs for non-network care. PPOs sometimes require members to meet a deductible (especially for hospitalization) and may have bigger copayments than HMOs.

Regardless of whether you have an HMO or a PPO, different policies have different coverage priorities. These include things like doctor visits, preventative care, diagnostic tests, hospital and extended care, emergency care, and prescription drugs. "Extra" coverage areas might include dental insurance, vision care, care by specialists, mental health care, services for drug/alcohol abuse, family planning services, chronic disease care, physical therapy, chiropractic care, and maternity care. You might be surprised to find out what is and isn't covered, so check.

If you do end up in the hospital, look your hospital bills over carefully to make sure they're right. An alarmingly high percentage of hospital bills have some type of error, so go over yours with a fine-toothed comb. You'd hate to be charged $7,000 instead of $70 because someone was a little keystroke happy. Be sure you know your coverage before you have anything done, and hang on to your explanation of benefits afterwards. Here are some of the more common billing mistakes to watch out for:

BASIC INFORMATION Be sure your name, address, health insurance provider, physician, and other basics are correct.

DUPLICATE BILLING Make sure you haven't been charged twice for the same service, supplies, or medications.

NUMBER OF DAYS IN HOSPITAL Check the dates of your admission and discharge. Were you charged for the discharge day? Most hospitals will charge for the day of admission, but not for the day of discharge.

INCORRECT ROOM CHARGES If you were in a semiprivate room, make sure you're not being charged for a private one.

OPERATING-ROOM TIME It's not uncommon for hospitals to bill for more time than you actually used. Compare the charge with your anesthesiologist's records.

UPCODING Hospitals sometimes shift the charge for a lower-cost service or medication to one that's more costly. For example, a doctor orders a generic drug, but the patient is charged for a pricier brand name.

KEYSTROKE ERROR A computer operator accidentally hits the wrong key on a keyboard. It can cost you hundreds of dollars and result in an incorrect charge for a service you didn't get.

CANCELED WORK Your physician ordered a test, and then cancelled it, but you were charged anyway.

SERVICES NEVER RENDERED Did you get every service, treatment, and medication for which you were charged?

AUTO INSURANCE

Remember how psyched you were to get your driver's license? Well, getting car insurance isn't nearly as fun, but you gotta do it. The majority of states require you to have auto insurance, and most require that you carry bodily injury liability and property damage liability insurance as well. The first step in choosing the insurance you want for your car is to know the laws in your state. This will tell you the minimum insurance you need for your car. Keep in mind that just because your state may not require extensive insurance, extra coverage may be worth the expense. After all, no one wants to be stuck with thousands of dollars worth of bills because of an auto accident.

Auto insurance is simply about how much you are willing to pay out of your own pocket versus how much you want the insurance company to cover. Once you decide this, you're ready to buy your auto insurance policy.

Before you seek out a policy, gather personal information about your driving history, car, and your current auto insurance. To find an insurance agent, ask friends and families who they use and consult the Yellow Pages. Call a couple of different companies for specific quotes—you might be surprised at how much you can save using a particular one. When asking about the types and rates of coverage they offer, ask about rental car coverage in case your car is in the shop and ask if towing is included in your policy.

Don't ever lie to insurance companies about where you live or who drives your car—they may not cover you if something happens. If you give a friend's address because auto insurance is less expensive for her zip code and then your car is broken into at your address, your insurance may deny you coverage. Same goes if you don't divulge all of the drivers of your car and then your friend crashes your car. (The easiest way to avoid losing your car *or* a friendship is to have a firm policy about not letting other people drive your car. Simply tell them your insurance doesn't cover them, regardless of whether or not it does.)

Requirements for coverage eligibility vary from company to company and state to state. Many insurance policies combine a number of types of coverage—here's a rundown of them:

COLLISION INSURANCE Reimburses you for the cost of repairs to your car as the result of a collision with another car or object.

COMPREHENSIVE INSURANCE Covers damage to your car from events other than an accident, such as fire, broken windshields, vandalism, theft, wind, falling objects, and hail.

LIABILITY INSURANCE Pays for accidental bodily injury and property damages to others. Injury damages include medical expenses, pain and suffering, and lost wages. Property damage includes damaged items and automobiles. This coverage also pays defense and court costs and protects you from personal injury lawsuits. It is now required in most states.

MEDICAL INSURANCE Pays medical expenses regardless of fault when the expenses are caused by an auto accident.

UNINSURED MOTORIST INSURANCE Pays your car's damages when an auto accident is caused by a driver who doesn't have liability insurance.

UNDERINSURED MOTORIST INSURANCE Pays your car's damages when an auto accident is caused by a driver who has insufficient liability insurance.

No matter what type of coverage you choose, you'll have a deductible to meet (the amount of money you pay out of your pocket before your insurance kicks in). Collision coverage deductibles usually range from $250-$1,000 a year, and comprehensive deductibles are about $100-$300. The higher your deductible, the lower your insurance, but make sure your deductible is low enough that you'll be able to pay it.

Auto insurance rates are based on your past driving performance, age, sex, marital status, where you live, and the kind of car you drive. The good news is women usually pay less than men, and many rates decline significantly once you reach age twenty-five.

If you live with your parents, you can get your auto insurance policy under theirs if they agree to it. If you're a college student living in another town, don't worry—you're usually still covered under your parent's policy until you're twenty-five.

Ask about discounts. You may qualify if you're accident-free, have antitheft devices (alarms, digital door locks, electronic tracking systems), are a good driver, are a good student, have had driver training, have multiple policy coverage, or have a car that "looks good" to insurance companies. "Looking good" doesn't mean it's a sweet ride. It means insurance companies know what kinds of cars are prone to problems and what kinds of cars are most often stolen. If you haven't bought your car yet, find out what cars make this "good list" among auto insurers.

RENTER'S INSURANCE

If you have your own place, your belongings can no longer be covered under your parents' homeowner's insurance and you need to purchase your own insurance. (If you are a college student and temporarily living somewhere, you might be covered under their insurance, but be sure to check their policy.) When thinking about renter's insurance, you have to decide how much personal stuff you've invested in and, if something happened, if you could you afford to replace it all yourself. Before you dismiss the idea because you think that your vintage Spice Girls CD collection isn't worth much money, think about how much your clothes and shoes alone would probably cost you to replace. Be sure to pay attention to whether a policy's coverage is *actual cash value* (what your stuff was worth at the time it was damaged or stolen) or *replacement cost coverage* (what it will really cost you to have it replaced today).

Although you wouldn't be responsible for damages to your apartment or building due to vandalism or natural disasters, you do have personal property—clothes, jewelry, furniture, electronic equipment, memorabilia—that you need to protect. Renter's insurance covers your belongings in case they are damaged due to fire, theft, water damage, smoke, and other disasters. Renter's insurance also protects you against liability if someone is injured in your apartment. It is important to note that a renter's policy may cover you from some events but not others: damage due to floods, hurricanes, and other disasters may not be covered under your policy, so read it carefully.

There are standard liability limits for several categories of things. For example, the loss or theft of coins or money is usually limited to $100; silverware, $1,000; guns, $1,000 to $2,000; jewelry, $1,000 to $2,000. A way to increase the categorical liability limits is to purchase a "rider" (addendum to the standard policy). So if Aunt Edith's gorgeous heirloom tanzanite ring is worth $5,000, you'd need an additional rider for the other $3,000-$4,000 to be fully covered. It's important to note that specialized riders often require an inspection by way of appraisal.

As with your other insurance, shop around for the best rates. Renter's insurance costs about $10-$15 a month, plus you'll still have a deductible (the amount you'll have to pay before coverage kicks in). But that's not much if you consider how much you'd spend replacing all of your lost things. You may even get a discount from your insurance agent if you have another insurance policy (such as auto) with him or her.

Ask your agent about other discounts too. Many companies reduce your rates if you have protective or preventative devices such as a smoke detector, burglar alarm, or fire extinguisher.

Once you obtain your policy, borrow a video camera and walk through your apartment to document all of your belongings. Open closets and drawers. Make a duplicate copy of this tape and keep one in a safe deposit box and one in another place, say at your parent's house.

LIFE INSURANCE

Thinking about life insurance is about as pleasant as having the dentist skip the Novocain when drilling your tooth, so I'll try to get through the subject as thoroughly and quickly as possible. Life insurance is necessary only for persons upon whom others are dependent for one reason or another. It provides instant liquidity to meet the obligations that become due upon your death.

If you're single and renting an apartment or house with no dependents, you probably don't need much if any life insurance. There is no one in your life dependent on your income. (Well, okay, maybe your cat, but that doesn't really qualify, so you can make arrangements for Tiger to go live with a family member or friends.) You could purchase a very small policy to pay for your funeral and burial, but that's about it.

If, on the other hand, you are a single person with a home mortgage, you may need life insurance to save your parents (or whomever else you have willed the house to) the problem of disposing of your estate. For example, imagine that you die and your parents inherit your house. They want to sell it but it sits on the market for two years, so they'll have to pay the mortgage for it. You might buy a policy to cover the expected payments over (for example) two years or the entire mortgage. And, of course, if you have a child, you will need life insurance to ensure his or her financial future.

There are other instances in which you might want to consider purchasing life insurance: If you have cosigned a loan with anyone, if you have a friend or relative to whom you want to leave money, if your parents won't be able to manage financially if you're not around, or if you want to leave money to a charity or other nonprofit organization.

Car Care Checklist

Some of these things you can do and check yourself. Others you might want to have a qualified mechanic do.

Check monthly:

✓ **OIL LEVEL**–Add oil if low (but don't overfill) and check for leaks.

✓ **HOSES**–Replace if bulging, rotten, or brittle.

✓ **BELTS**–Replace if worn or frayed.

✓ **TIRE PRESSURE**–Add air if low.

✓ **COOLANT OR ANTIFREEZE**–Add more if low.

✓ **AIR FILTER**–Replace if dirty or at recommended mileage intervals.

✓ **TIRES**–Inspect for leaks, damage, bulges, or uneven wear.

Check every three months:

✓ **OIL AND OIL FILTER**–Change every 3,000 miles or as recommended by manufacturer.

✓ **FLUIDS**–Add windshield washer fluid, battery and power steering fluid, brake fluid, and transmission fluid if low, and look for leaks.

✓ **BATTERY TERMINALS AND CABLES**–Clean if corroded.

Check every six months:

✓ **WIPER BLADES**–Replace if worn, brittle, or smeary.

✓ **LIGHTS**–Make sure headlights, tail lights, brake lights, interior lights, and turn signals work.

✓ **HORN**–Make sure works properly.

✓ **BRAKES**–Inspect for wear and tear.

✓ **SPARE TIRE**–Make sure is fully inflated.

✓ **EXHAUST SYSTEM**–Inspect for rust, damage, or loose parts.

✓ **SHOCK ABSORBERS**–Inspect for oil seepage or wear.

CAR CRISES

You don't have to be Ms. Goodwrench to keep your car hum-
ming along. Simply keeping an eye on some of its basic compo-
nents can help you avoid breakdowns and save money. Review
your owner's manual to familiarize yourself with your car and
check the manufacturer's recommendations. You'll need to have
your car regularly serviced by a qualified technician in accor-
dance to the manufacturer's recommendations, but the Car Care
Checklist sidebar will give you some guidelines as to what you
should check and when.

Having your car serviced regularly and keeping it maintained
will help ward off big uh-ohs. There are also sights, sounds, and
smells that indicate there could be a problem. Pull over to a safe
spot, stop your car immediately, turn off the engine, and turn
your hazards on if:

* **A warning light remains on**
* **You feel any unusual vibrations**
* **Your temperature gauge
  reads hot**
* **You hear any unusual noises, rattling, or grindings**
* **Your oil pressure gauge
  reads low**
* **Your vehicle has a tendency
  to wander or steer to
  one side**
* **You experience any abnormalities when braking.**

You should also get your car to a mechanic as soon as possible if it's difficult to start, uses more fuel or oil than usual, runs roughly, leaves oil or coolant on the driveway, or blows smoke.

If you think a good man is hard to find, a good mechanic is even harder. But don't despair—they're out there. I think word of mouth is the best method for finding a good mechanic, so ask around and see who has had consistently satisfactory work done by their mechanic. It's best to talk to someone with a car similar to yours. Start your search before you have a major crises with your vehicle, and test out a potential mechanic with a small job like an oil change.

Junk in the Trunk

Whether you're traveling ten miles or 10,000 miles, you should always be prepared in case of an accident, breakdown, inclement weather, or other hazard. Here are some things to keep in your car:

- Proof of insurance card and registration
- Owner's manual
- Disposable camera (for taking pictures at the scene of an accident)
- Pad of paper and pen
- Flashlight
- Cell phone and charger
- Jumper cables
- Bag of salt or kitty litter in the winter if your car is rear-wheel drive (keep in the trunk to add weight and keep your car from sliding)
- Windshield scraper
- Bottled water
- Toolbox
- Blanket
- Warm clothes
- A pair of boots (in case you have to get out and push or walk)
- First-aid kit
- Latex gloves (in case you need to help someone who is injured)
- Old towel(s) and rags
- Flares
- A funnel (in case you need to add fluids to your car)
- Non-perishable food (e.g., PowerBars)

It's good to know what's covered under warranty so you don't pay for something the manufacturer should. If it isn't covered, always get an estimate—and approve it—*before* a mechanic proceeds with the repair. If you're in doubt as to their estimate or the amount of work they say needs to be done, get a second opinion and see how the two compare. Do be cautious about an exceptionally low price—the parts or labor may not be reliable. You can always make a call to the Better Business Bureau.

If you're in a car accident, the first thing you need to do is stop and move your car out of the way. If you don't stop you'll be in big trouble with the law. Turn your car off to avoid a possible fire. Make sure that no one is hurt. If they are, call 911 immediately and don't move them. Call the police. Sometimes they won't come to the scene if there isn't an injury, but you want to make sure authorities document your call, and you'll need to file a police report. Take pictures with a disposable camera (see the Junk in the Trunk sidebar), or if your cell phone has a camera function, use it.

Pay close attention to and take notes on everything that happens at the scene of an accident. Exchange names, addresses, telephone numbers, driver's licenses, license plate numbers, and insurance information with the other driver(s) involved. If there are any witnesses, get the same information from them. Call your insurance agent. Whatever you do, don't admit fault. Keep your comments to yourself and let the insurance companies and police settle it.

APARTMENT ANTICS

Blown fuses, stuck thermostats, and clogged toilets—ahhhh the glamorous side of living on your own. Keeping a list of emergency telephone numbers (utility companies, poison control, your apartment manager, maintenance, maintenance after-hours, your doctor, the nearest hospital, family and close friends) posted inside a kitchen cabinet will help so that you're not scrambling through the phonebook when you need to make a call quickly. Also, it's a good idea to know where things are located and have supplies on hand before you have a problem.

THE ELECTRICITY GOES OUT

First, unplug your computer, TV set, stereo, and any other valuable electronics. Sometimes during a storm, there will be power surges which cause wide fluctuations in line voltage. These can be destructive to

Tool Time

Put together a basic toolbox or designate a tool drawer or shelf. (Even though it won't fit in your toolbox, a toilet plunger is also a good thing to have on hand.) Include:

- Hammer
- Assortment of nails and hangers
- Thumbtacks
- Tape (scotch, masking, duct, and electrical)
- Glue (Elmer's, Super, and glue gun sticks)
- Glue gun
- Safety pins
- Sandpaper
- Screwdriver (Phillips and flathead)
- String
- Tape measure
- Flashlight
- Adjustable wrench
- Batteries (AAA, AA, D, and 9 volt)
- Pliers
- Swiss Army knife
- Utility knife (with a razor blade)
- Scissors
- Pen and pad of paper

electronics. (You should also have a surge protected power strip on your electronics.)

Take a look around. If your entire apartment complex or neighborhood is black, it's probably out of your control. Call the electric company from a cell phone or a phone with a cord.

If you think you're the only one without electricity, you may have just blown a fuse or jumped a breaker. Before a blackout, know where your breaker box or fuse box is; usually it's in a hall closet of an apartment or the basement, garage, or laundry room of a house. (A breaker box has a small metal door that when opened has a series of over-sized looking light switches.) All of the switches should be going the same way, so if one isn't, turn it off, and then flip it so that it's going the same way as the rest of the switches. Fuses must be replaced.

If the electricity goes out, be ready with flashlights (and batteries); keep them in your nightstand and in the kitchen. Candles and matches are also good to have on hand, as is a good old-fashioned non-cordless phone—your cordless one won't work if there's an electrical power failure. Simply unplug your cordless one from the phone jack and plug in your old one.

YOU SMELL NATURAL GAS

Natural gas has no odor, but a harmless chemical (mercaptan) is added to give it a rotten egg smell it so that you can smell it. If you smell this, *don't* flip on any electrical switches, turn on any appliances, pull any plugs from their outlets, use the telephone, or light any matches. It could ignite the gas and cause an explosion. Leave your apartment immediately (taking your pet with you) and call the gas company from a safe location.

A TORNADO OR HURRICANE HITS

In either case, the lower the better, so if you have plenty of warning, go to a friend's house with a basement; if not, this is the perfect excuse to get to know that cute guy on the first floor. Or, if your apartment complex has a laundry room on a lower floor, go there. If you're inside an apartment, go to the most interior room—probably the bathroom—away from any windows where you could get hit with glass or debris. Wrap up in a blanket (again to protect yourself from any debris) and cover your head. Keep a radio with batteries, a flashlight, a cell phone, and bottled water nearby.

FIRE STRIKES

Know where the fire exits are in your building, plan how you'd escape from each room, check your smoke detector once a month, change the batteries twice a year (in the fall and spring when you change your clock), and keep a fire extinguisher handy. Don't overload your electrical outlets and remember to put out any candles that you light.

If a fire in your apartment is out of your control, get out fast. Check doors to see if there is smoke and feel them to see if they are warm. If you can't get out of your apartment, call 911 and tell them where you are. Go out to the balcony (but *not* the roof) and wave your arms wildly and yell. If you can't get outside, wet towels and stuff them in vents and around the bottom of doors. Wherever you are, stay low—smoke rises.

If you can get out of your apartment, leave and yell, "Fire!" to alert others that they need to leave too. If there's a fire alarm in the stairwell or outside, pull it. Call the fire department when you reach a safe area.

In addition to the above-mentioned scenarios, you may also encounter some minor problems inside your apartment. If you're renting your place, there should be a maintenance man on duty. If you're really lucky, there's one on call even after hours. But if not, don't despair. The following are some common problems you might encounter and ways you can handle them until there's help.

THE TOILET CLOGS

Flush—once. Any more than this and you'll probably just end up all wet. Let the water drain down as much as possible, and then stick a plunger in the toilet. Put it over the hole and make sure it fits tightly around it while plunging up and down a few times. If there's room in the toilet, pour some boiling water in and try plunging again. If your toilet overflows, look for the cutoff valve near the tank and turn the water off.

THE TOILET WON'T STOP RUNNING

It's not only annoying listening to a running toilet, but it will add to your water bill too. First, try to simply jiggle—not flush—the handle on the toilet and wait a couple of minutes. If this doesn't work, lift off the tank lid (careful—it's heavy). Look at the chain and make sure it's not knotted, twisted, or caught under the stopper. If it isn't the chain, it could be a worn stopper or seal that needs to be replaced by maintenance.

THE SINK OR SHOWER DRAIN IS STOPPED UP

Most clogs are caused by clumps of hair (I know—ewww, gross). If you can't fish the clump out by hand, unbend a wire coat hanger until it's straight and try to fish it out.

THE THERMOSTAT DOESN'T WORK

Call maintenance. Unless you have a degree in engineering, you probably won't be able to fix this one yourself. If the heat is broken, snuggle under blankets with your man or your cat and layer your clothes. If doors and windows aren't sealed well, put towels underneath to help keep cold air out. If you live in a really cold climate, an electric blanket might be a good investment.

If the air conditioning is broken, get some air moving with electric fans. Wear lightweight, loose-fitting, light-colored clothing, and drink plenty of water. If you get too uncomfortable, bunk in with a friend who has air conditioning.

A MAJOR KITCHEN APPLIANCE BREAKS

Call the maintenance man; your landlord should fix or replace the appliance at no charge to you. If it's the fridge, try to salvage perishables in a cooler with ice. If it's the oven or stovetop, well, enjoy dinner out!

PROTECT YOURSELF

I love the way Sydney Bristow kicks butt on the TV show *Alias*. Now, okay, maybe you're not a trained government secret agent, but you can minimize your chances of being a target *and* reduce the likelihood of being a victim. There is no cookie-cutter answer for the type of hazard you encounter. Only you have all of the information in the situation, so keep your cool and trust your gut so that you can make an intelligent decision quickly.

GO WITH YOUR GUT

If you feel apprehensive, anxious, suspicious, or fearful in a particular situation, figure out why. Maybe it's nothing, but if you dismiss your feelings entirely, you may defeat your best defense system and unknowingly help in your own victimization.

BE PREPARED

Carry a cell phone and keep it charged and handy. Keep gas in your car and your car maintained so you don't end up stuck late at night in an undesirable part of town. Always have cash in your wallet to avoid unexpected ATM trips. Have a telephone in the bedroom. Have your keys in your hand and poking out between your fingers so that you're ready to open your car or apartment as soon as you reach it and aren't fumbling around in your purse.

BE AWARE OF YOUR SURROUNDINGS

Walk briskly with your head held high. Convey your best don't-mess-with-me attitude and they probably won't. You really shouldn't jog outside with headphones on, but if you do, wear your headphones so that they're not totally covering your ears and you can still hear surrounding noises. As you approach your car look around and under it to ensure there is no one there, and before you unlock the door, check the backseat to make sure no one is crouching down. Once in your car, lock your doors, turn the ignition key, and drive. This is not the time to inspect your makeup or fiddle with the radio.

BE ESPECIALLY VIGILANT
DURING WARM WEATHER MONTHS

According to the FBI, July and August consistently report the highest rates of rape and aggravated assault, probably because more people are outside then, increasing the number of potential victims.

DON'T CARRY A WEAPON

A weapon is no help unless you know how to use it and are prepared to do so. Even mace. Remember that if you don't use your weapon, it can be grabbed and used against you.

PARK IN WELL-LIT AREAS

Even if you have to pay, it's worth it. If you're leaving your office late, arrange to move your car as close to the exit as possible when all the other employees leave to go home. Have security walk you to your car. Asking for an escort is not a sign of weakness—it's a sign of being smart.

SAFETY IN NUMBERS

Don't walk alone. If you're with a group of friends, ask a male friend (no, not a guy you just met at the bar—someone you know well and trust) to escort you home. You're not being a damsel in distress, you're *preventing* yourself from being a damsel in distress.

LEAVE YOURSELF AN OUT

Try to stay an equal distance from the curb and buildings when you're on the sidewalk in an urban area. Crimes involving perpetrators in cars or on bikes occur close to the curb and many abductions occur near buildings and alleyways.

GIVE UP THE GOODS

Never risk your personal safety over your purse, jewelry, or car. Give him the material stuff he wants.

DON'T BE NICE

As women, we tend to be pleasers. But being nice to a stranger can get you hurt. Be wary of unsolicited promises ("Don't worry, I won't hurt you"), forced camaraderie ("How are we going to fix this flat tire?"), pleas for help ("I've sprained my ankle—can you help me?"), and refusals to hear the word "no." If you think someone legitimately needs help, call the police and let them be the Boy Scout.

HAVE A CHECK-IN SYSTEM

This is especially important if you live by yourself. As I mentioned in chapter 3, my girlfriends and I did this. Even though we were usually calling to divulge the latest dating disaster or bit of office gossip, it was still a good way to make sure we were all accounted for.

TAKE A SELF-DEFENSE COURSE

A good self-defense program should offer options, techniques, and ways of analyzing situations. Check with police, rape crisis centers, the YMCA/YWCA, local colleges, and martial arts schools to find a place that offers classes.

REMEMBER THE DETAILS

If you find yourself a victim of an attack, try to remember details about him: facial features, race, eye color, scars, tattoos, hairstyle, and clothing colors and styles. Also try and recall his mode of transportation, and if it's a car, the color and brand of car and the license plate number (chunking it into two smaller separate numbers is easier). It would be tough for an attacker to change *all* of these things about himself.

HAVE A VAGUE OUTGOING
MESSAGE ON YOUR ANSWERING MACHINE

Give as few clues as possible about who lives there. Use "we" instead of "I" even if you live alone so that it doesn't appear as though you do. Consider having a male's voice leave the message. A message such as, "Hi this is Liz, I'm on vacation until June 30" isn't a helpful voicemail, it's an invitation to be a victim.

SECURE YOUR PLACE

Make sure all of your home's doors and windows are locked and establish a routine so you remember to do these things every day. Be sure that areas around your house are well-lit and leave a light on inside when you go out. Not only will it be easier for you to get inside, but a lot of light may also ward off would-be burglars because they don't want to be seen. Don't leave a spare key under the doormat or flowerpot—that's the first place a would-be burglar looks. If you see someone hanging around or something that doesn't look right, call the police.

Don't put valuables where they are easily seen from a window. And don't laugh, but consider hiding any valuable jewelry in a tampon box under the sink in the bathroom. Most burglars will not be interested in perusing your feminine hygiene products. Just don't throw the box away!

GET TO KNOW YOUR NEIGHBORS

Know who should be there so you can spot who shouldn't. Get to know routines and look out for one another when you're gone. Collect each other's mail and papers and keep an eye on the place so you aren't an easy target for a burglar.

AVOID IDENTITY THEFT

Make sure your incoming and outgoing e-mail and snail mail is safe. Keep track of monthly statements so you'll notice anything odd right away. Use unusual passwords, such as a childhood pet combined with your mother's maiden name. Carry just one credit card. Tear up forms or statements that have identifying information like your Social Security number. Consider using a shredder. Be careful where you put your things and your purse, even if it is in your office at work. Be smart about to whom you dole out personal information. And finally, review your credit report from time to time.

GETTING PINK-SLIPPED

You hear the words, "You're fired!" but they didn't come from The Donald and it's anything but TV-viewing pleasure. And you most likely won't get your own talk show, clothing line, or book deal.

If the dot.com industry showed us anything few years ago, it's that layoffs can happen to anyone at any company, in any industry, at any time. It's not a cause for shame or necessarily a result of your performance. No matter how responsible you are, you may find yourself out of a job at some point in your life. A lot of what I mentioned in chapter 1 will again apply here. And there are some other things you can do in case you find yourself clearing out your cubicle.

FILE FOR UNEMPLOYMENT

File for benefits at the closest unemployment office as soon as possible. Check your state employment commission and understand the law. Several states allow you to work some hours during the week and still collect unemployment. There can be a delay on receiving the first check, so file right away. Don't count on a severance package, especially if your company goes broke. Going out of business goes hand in hand with running out of cash.

RETHINK YOUR EXPENSES

Find ways to trim your budget and prioritize debt. Dip into your emergency savings fund if need be to keep up your fixed expenses like insurance premiums, installment payments, rent, and any other payments due on a specific date. Car payments and mortgages should be a priority because these loans are backed by collateral and creditors can take away your home or car. Call creditors and explain your situation and see if they'll work with you.

CONTINUE YOUR HEALTH INSURANCE

If you had health insurance through your employer, you're allowed to continue the policy you had while employed thanks to COBRA (a federal law that lets individuals continue their health insurance policy when they lose or leave a job). You're allowed to pay group rates plus a set administrative fee, usually for up to eighteen months. So, you'll pay more than you were paying for the premiums when the company was also kicking in, but at least you'll still be covered.

GET A JOB

Wait tables, work retail, substitute teach. You still have to pay your bills, and having a job to go to will get you out of bed, provide structure, keep you from wallowing in self-pity, and keep you motivated to work.

KEEP YOUR RÉSUMÉ UPDATED

Don't wait until you're axed to start putting one together. Even if you have a great career and plan to stay at your company forever, you can never get too comfortable. Besides, you never know when you'll want to apply for a board position, a committee, or your dream job, so it's a good idea to always keep your résumé updated and on hand.

KEEP CONTACTS WARM

Go to conferences, do favors for former colleagues, and let everyone know you're looking. If your company downsized, stay in touch with other colleagues who were laid off and keep track of where they went afterward. There may be opportunities for you there too. Even if it feels awkward, try hard to keep relationships with your boss and those higher up in good repair.

AVOID A RÉSUMÉ GAP

It's important to show employers you've stayed productive between jobs. Take a class in your field, upgrade your skills, volunteer with an organization, write an article in your area of expertise, and hobnob with your network of industry contacts.

SET YOUR SITES (A LITTLE) LOWER

If you've been laid off in an unstable industry, you may

have to scale back your salary expectations (and your ego) and be a little more realistic. If the market for high-paying positions in your field no longer exists, you may need to consider looking for a lower-paying position.

HAVE A ROUTINE

To keep your spirits up and be productive, structure your day like a workday. Don't just move from your bed to the couch to watch a *Real World* marathon. Get up, have coffee, read the paper, and go to work—finding a job.

BE GOOD TO YOURSELF

Eat a proper diet, work out, get plenty of sleep, and take time to enjoy life. Build a strong support system of family and friends or anyone else who will cheer you up when you feel down. Remember—this is just a small pothole on your fabulous road trip of life.

What things can you do or classes can you take to protect yourself?

....

....

....

....

....

....

....

....

TO DO! Take care of your car with this checklist . . .

....

....

....

....

....

....

....

TO DO! Here are some toolbox essentials . . .

....

....

....

....

....

....

CHEAT SHEET! Important telephone numbers to have on hand . . .

....

....

....

....

....

....

....

FINAL WORD

I hope I've given you some guidance on how to live fabulously and frugally as you journey out on your own. Keep going, embrace life, and live it to the fullest. Whatever challenges you face, I know you'll have the cleverness and chutzpah to overcome them.

Happy chick living!

ABOUT THE AUTHOR

 Kris Koederitz Melcher is a former public relations account executive for an international public relations firm. She has written, pitched, and placed articles in such venues as *PARADE Magazine, USA Weekend, Ladies' Home Journal, Working Mother, New Woman, Parents, Modern Bride, Woman's Day, Better Homes and Gardens, Midwest Living, House Beautiful,* and *For the Bride by Demetrios.* She is a graduate of the University of Missouri School of Journalism. In her spare time, she enjoys flying, scuba diving, boating, entertaining, wine tasting, and running. She strives to live a fabulous and frugal lifestyle in Leawood, Kansas, with her husband Jeff and daughter Isabella.

Visit her at *www.chickliving.com.*